WHAT LEADERS ARE SAYING
ABOUT
RE-VISIONING

I've had the joy of being a part of Seacoast Church for the past 26 years as it has grown from a single location with a few hundred people to a multi-site church reaching tens of thousands. My pastor, Greg Surratt, has been a steady leader through it all, offering sound advice and encouragement as the seasons of our church have changed and as his leadership has grown. He is a champion mentor, a pastor to pastors, a practical wisdom-giver, and joyful peddler of hope. This book will help you remember you are not alone on your leadership journey and give you the courage to experience "re-visioning" in your church or ministry.

TARA BANKS
Worship Pastor, Seacoast Church
Charleston, South Carolina

This book is classic Greg Surratt. All of us wrestle with the tension between high expectations and seasons of disappointment. As I read Greg's book, I wasn't surprised that sometimes he has wanted to quit, but I was surprised that he was honest enough to tell us about it! No matter where we are in our careers, all of us need gentle (and sometimes not-so-gentle) reminders that all we do is a response to the grace and greatness of Jesus. I wholeheartedly recommend this book!

RANDY BEZET

Lead Pastor, Bayside Community Church

Bradenton, Florida

Greg Surratt is a great listener and a real friend. If Pastor Greg is talking, I'll always lean in. He's one of those men who brings a timely word, enormous grace, and healthy accountability when you need it the most. In *Re-Visioning*, Pastor Greg does a fantastic job of communicating in a way that you'll feel like he's reading your mail, and then pouring his huge heart of compassion and understanding all over you. If you soak in his tested wisdom, you'll be strengthened and encouraged.

RICK BEZET

Lead Pastor, New Life Church of Arkansas and co-author of *Real Love* and *Be Real*

Little Rock, Arkansas and other sites

Limits are real. Some are unavoidable, but most of them are self-imposed. The ones we put on ourselves and God are truly the ones that hurt us. I'm so glad that Greg Surratt was bold enough to encourage us to live beyond the limits. Through humor, insight, and life experience, *Re-Visioning* will help you move from limited to limitless.

MICAHN CARTER

Lead Pastor of Together Church and author, *Made for The Middle*

Yakima, Washington

To know Greg Surratt is to love him! For 17 years, I've watched him encourage and inspire leaders like no other. This book is him, in written form. It's hard to learn from people who've been overnight successes, which is why *Re-Visioning: How to Stay Sharp at Every Stage of Your Church's Life* is so refreshing. With honesty and humor, Greg shares the struggles and limitations he's endured on his ministry journey. It will not only make you a better leader, but it will lift your spirits and enlarge your vision!

JOE CHAMPION

Senior Pastor of Celebration Church

Austin, Texas

Drift. It's a killer. Pastors bear tremendous responsibility for their leaders, their flocks, and their communities. The weight we carry as pastors can slowly crush the spiritual vitality out of us—if we don't have a plan. Greg Surratt knows this pressure, and in *Re-Visioning: How to Stay Sharp at Every Stage of Your Church's Life*, he refreshes our calling and reminds us that it's worth it. But that's not all—Greg gives us real, practical solutions to keep us on track and fight the drift. I wholeheartedly recommend this book!

HERBERT COOPER

Senior Pastor of People's Church and author of *But God Changes Everything*

Oklahoma City, Oklahoma

Greg Surratt is a friend to me and many other pastors; but more than that, he's a mentor to so many of us. In his new book, *Re-Visioning*, Greg will mentor you through heartwarming stories, powerful principles and clear applications. This is a book that will clarify your direction while bringing you joy and courage.

DAVE FERGUSON

Lead Pastor, Community Christian Church and author of *Hero Maker: Five Essential Practices for Leaders to Multiply Leaders*

Chicago, Illinois

This book is a "must read" for pastors and leaders at every level, whether you've been pastoring 35 years for just stepped into your first ministry role. There is inspiration, encouragement, and instruction on every page. Greg's grace-filled, faith-producing, down-to-earth style is easy to absorb and makes this book a fast-paced treasure trove of wisdom. I'm buying a copy for everyone on my staff!

MICHAEL FLETCHER
Senior Pastor, Manna Church,
Fayetteville, North Carolina

Greg has been a lifelong friend since the early years of C3. When I was discouraged and didn't know who else to call, I called Greg. He encouraged me and spoke truth to me. No matter how hard truth was to hear, I always left the conversation with more wisdom and optimism than before I called him. Think of this book as a conversation with Greg. You might just need some truth and encouragement today, and you'll find that in these pages. I highly recommend this book to every leader.

MATT FRY
Lead Pastor, C3 Church
Clayton, North Carolina

If I've learned anything about pastoring in 47 years of ministry, I've learned that we all "hit the wall" at some time or another. In *Re-Visioning*, Greg Surratt shows us that we all make critical mistakes, but by making adjustments, we can renew our passions and infuse new life into our local churches. Follow the guy who has done it over the long-haul!

WILLIE GEORGE
Founding Pastor, Church on the Move
Tulsa, Oklahoma

Many pastors struggle to overcome trials and setbacks in their ministry. *Re-Visioning: How to Stay Sharp at Every Stage of Your Church's Life* will not only help you survive ministry, but empower you to do it sustainably, effectively, and with joy. Pastor Greg Surratt is overflowing with useful thoughts and big ideas gained from decades of experience in church leadership. If you want to tear down the walls that keep you from pursuing God's calling, read this book!

CRAIG GROESCHEL

Senior Pastor, Life.Church and *New York Times* bestselling author

Edmond, Oklahoma

Greg Surratt is a pastor's pastor and knows how to encourage our hearts and refresh our spirits as we seek to serve the Lord. Filled with his usual wit, wisdom, and wonderful insight into Scripture, *Re-Visioning—How to Stay Sharp at Every Stage of Your Church's Life* reminds us that we all struggle, no matter how large or small our churches or how long we've been in ministry. Leaders young and old will return to this book again and again for its deeply encouraging message of hope, power, and renewal.

CHRIS HODGES

Senior Pastor, Church of the Highlands and author of *The Daniel Dilemma* and
What's Next?

Birmingham, Alabama

There are few ministers with the experience and expertise to navigate seasons of ministry better than Greg. He not only has navigated them; he's successfully stayed on point even when facing the many obstacles all of us face in ministry. He is beloved by his family, staff, and countless friends and leaders who have experienced his counsel and encouragement in guiding them on their journeys to become everything God has created them to be.

He's an outstanding leader and pastor! Wherever you are in your leadership and your church's journey, this is a must-have book from a spiritual giant of the faith who has walked the same paths you have walked and has been successful at every stage of life and ministry.

CRAIG JOHNSON

Senior Director of Ministries at Lakewood Church and Founder of Champions Clubs

Houston, Texas

Greg Surratt is a pioneer in church planting and multi-site strategy. Leaders in all sizes of churches and across the spectrum of denominations value his insights, his heart, and his blend of kindness and tenacity in advancing God's kingdom. Some of us are just starting out in pastoral leadership, but many of us have been around the block several times. From time to time, all of us need a trusted friend to put his arm around us and encourage us... or maybe give us a nudge in the right direction. Greg is that kind of friend. I'm grateful to him for sharing his heart with us.

ROB KETTERLING

Lead Pastor, River Valley Church and author of *Fix It! Whose Problem Is It?*

Apple Valley, Minnesota

Through *Re-Visioning*, many more church leaders will experience the benefits of Greg's wisdom, love, and humor. His stories are powerful, and his insights are profound. Read this book and give it to every leader who needs a refreshed vision...which is all of us.

MILES MCPHERSON

Senior Pastor of Rock Church and author of *The Third Option – Hope for a Racially Divided Nation*

San Diego, California

Greg has been a leader of leaders for as long as I have had the privilege of knowing him. This makes him more than qualified to write this particular book. The enemy will do anything to make the church ineffective. We must all lay down our pride and learn from each other with vulnerability. This book helps in that journey.

DAVID L. MEYER
CEO of Hand of Hope, Joyce Meyer Ministries World Missions
St. Louis, Missouri

This book had me hooked right from the beginning. Greg's humor and wisdom sets the stage to help us lead ourselves better so we can lead others well. He deals with the issues we all face in ministry, and he gives us hope and the tools to envision our future. No matter where you are on your journey of pastoral leadership, *Re-Visioning* will encourage you to keep moving forward.

TODD MULLINS
Senior Pastor, Christ Fellowship Church
West Palm Beach, Florida

Think Differently. Many times, this is a task that seems too big to accomplish. Greg has an incredible gift, to not only inspire but to cause you to think differently—to think and dream bigger. He truly is a gift to the body of Christ, and I'm so grateful for the relevant voice he carries for our generation. This book will give you insight and practical "how to" steps to clarify "the win" and attain the previously unattainable. Many times we embrace limitations that we put on ourselves, and we are convinced that they are immovable, when in reality, limitations can be lifted as we grow as a leader and stretch our thinking to see people the way Jesus sees them. Greg's life is testimony to what it looks like to be willing to adjust our perspective and personal preferences, and in doing so, reach more people more effectively, fulfilling the Great Commission in a generation desperately in need of more relevant leaders.

SHAUN NEPSTAD
Lead Pastor, Fellowship Church
Antioch and Lafayette, California

Greg Surratt has practiced what he has written. Here is a man who has been faithful to God's call for over 30 years. I have personally experienced his "sharpening" in my life and will never be the same because of it. He is a trusted guide to help leaders navigate both what's now and what's next in life and church leadership.

DARRIN PATRICK
Teaching Pastor, Seacoast Church and author of *Dude's Guide to Marriage*
Charleston, South Carolina

For more more than twenty years now, I've been blessed to have Greg Surratt in my life as a friend, an example to follow, an encourager, and an inspiration. For him to write a book on this topic is simply gold for pastors. His heart and wisdom and experience in ministry and the passion he has for helping other pastors - it all adds up to making his voice one of the tremendous assets in the Church today. If you're a pastor or leader, I'm convinced this book could make all the difference for you regardless of what season you're in.

DINO RIZZO
ARC Executive Director, Associate Pastor at Church of the Highlands
Author of *Servolution* and *Serve Your City*
Birmingham, Alabama

It's one thing to pastor a large church. It's quite another to pastor pastors. Pastor Greg Surratt is one of those people God uses to do both. In *Re-Visioning*, he pours his decades of experience into every page and every principle. If ministry and life have dulled you down, dive into this book . . . today. You won't regret it. Let Greg help you stay sharp.

STEVE ROBINSON
Senior Pastor, Church of the King
Mandeville, Louisiana

Pastor Greg is a catalyst who has inspires pastors around the world to reinvest in their dreams, see possibility where there is a challenge, and reimagine the possibilities for their big ideas. Every page of this book is filled with his wisdom, humor and advice, and he inspires you to keep moving forward with hope when you want to give up. *Re-Visioning* is a must read.

KATHY ROSEBOROUGH
Executive Assistant to Greg Surratt
Charleston, South Carolina

Greg is well-placed to write this book. As the founding pastor of Seacoast Church and President of ARC, he not only has huge experience and a proven track record, but also a wonderful combination of leadership wisdom, humility, humor and compassion for fellow pastors. There were so many helpful chapters. In each of them, I found the Lord ministering to me to keep pressing forward in all the seasons of life and ministry. Thank you, Greg. You're such a blessing!

DAVE SMITH
Senior Leader, KingsGate Community Church
Peterborough, United Kingdom

Re-visioning will sharpen your sword and encourage your heart. Greg's authenticity in sharing and his sincerity—along with years of experience—represent important facets that can inform our leadership journey and church trajectory. Each of the seven chapters and their respective questions deal with important truths every Christian leader needs to hear. As you hear from Greg's heart, be open to what God has to say to you.

ED STETZER

Billy Graham Distinguished Chair, Wheaton College

Wheaton, Illinois

Fathering is the most critical need in the body of Christ today, and fathering is Greg Surratt's heart. With over 800 ARC churches birthed from his church planting vision, his heart is for the precious pastors he works with. He even donated all the proceeds of this book to them! Follow Greg's wisdom. Follow Greg's example. Follow Greg's vision. If you have to follow someone, it might as well be someone who is "the real deal." This book flows directly from a heart of love...for YOU as a pastor.

LARRY STOCKSTILL

Teaching Pastor, Bethany Church

Baton Rouge, Louisiana

We all have seasons in ministry when we aren't sure we have it in us to keep pressing on. That's why we need friends who will help us stay focused when all we want to do is give up. They are fellow journeyman who will share honestly from their own places of discouragement while also giving us the hope we need to keep walking out our assignments from God. That's why I'm so thankful for Pastor Greg Surratt's book, *Re-Visioning*. If you've caught yourself daydreaming about running away from your calling, read this book. You'll be linking arms with a friend who will help you start moving forward once again with a renewed sense of purpose and hope.

LYSA TERKEURST

President, Proverbs 31 Ministries and #1 *New York Times* best-selling author

Charlotte, North Carolina

Greg Surratt has brought a word that every leader in every organization needs. The idea of long-term vision, culture and fruitfulness should be on all our minds. Greg will help you think through the process of reinventing yourself and creating a culture that will help you move forward. When we avoid these issues, death to the organization is inevitable. We either change, or we walk to a slow death. Greg brings life, fresh air and steps to help you get there. Read it. Your need it and you'll love it.

CASEY TREAT

Founder & Senior Pastor, Christian Faith

Seattle, Washington

I have often spoken to Greg Surratt about ideas, problems or decisions that I face as a pastor and leader, and he always has some great wisdom and insight about leadership and life. I consider Greg as a pastor's mentor, and even a pastor's best friend. In *Re-Visioning: How to Stay Sharp at Every Stage of Your Church's Life*, he reminds us why we got into ministry in the first place. His chapter on "Uncovering Hidden Desires" is one of my favorites. He describes how God patiently and powerfully took him through a process to rekindle his love for Jesus and his experience of God's presence. That chapter is worth the price of the book!

PHILIP WAGNER

Senior Pastor, Oasis Church LA, founder of Generosity.org and author of *Unlock Your Dream: Discover the Adventure you were created for*

Los Angeles, California

arc RESOURCES

HOW-TO SERIES

RE-VISIONING

*HOW TO STAY SHARP AT EVERY STAGE
OF YOUR CHURCH'S LIFE*

GREG SURRATT
FOREWORD BY SENATOR TIM SCOTT

DEDICATION

This book is dedicated to my friend and fellow dreamer, Billy Hornsby. Someone said: *"A friend is someone who knows the song in your heart and can sing it back to you when you've forgotten the words."*

You were that and more.

Gone but never forgotten. Your work lives on.

ISBN: 978-1-64296-012-9
Published by ARC, The Association of Related Churches
First printing 2019
Printed in the United States

Photos throughout the book were taken by Greg Surratt or are from his personal archives.

100% OF THE PROFITS FROM THIS BOOK GO TOWARD PLANTING CHURCHES THROUGH THE ASSOCIATION OF RELATED CHURCHES.

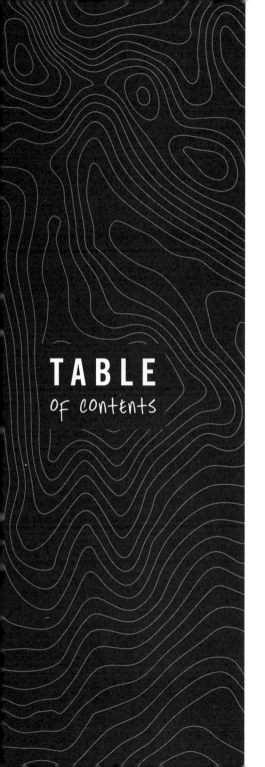

TABLE
of contents

FOREWORD

by Senator Tim Scott

In 1997, I had just been elected to the Charleston County Council. I was a babe in my political career, and I knew I needed someone to serve as a friend, spiritual advisor, and mentor. I asked Pastor Greg if he would be willing to play that role in my life, and he agreed. Soon, he completely changed my concept of "having lunch" with someone! Week after week, he instilled a biblical worldview that I could apply to the political and business worlds. I had been a Christian for many years, but my time with Greg drilled those principles much deeper into my life.

I believe that local service is where politicians cut their teeth so they can understand how their policies affect their constituents' daily lives and fulfill their hopes and dreams. This concept is consistent with the biblical view of leaders being servants and caring for the needs of those who are less fortunate. Over the years, Greg's input has clarified these perspectives and encouraged me to always have meaningful relationships with every strata in society.

Greg is a terrific mentor and a phenomenal leader. When I joined Seacoast, there were about a thousand people attending, and now there are about twenty thousand. For ten years, I was fortunate enough to have a catbird seat on the Board of Trustees and watch Greg as he built the church. I had been familiar with Proverbs 29:18, "Where there is no vision, the people are unrestrained." From my vantage point, I saw Greg get a vision from God and trust Him to bring it to reality regarding every aspect of Seacoast's exponential growth, as well as expanding to multi-site and church planting. But these aren't just numbers—the people at Seacoast are creating a vibrant community of faith and having an impact in the city to care for people in need.

As an elected official who tries to serve our state and the nation with honor, and as a former business owner, I've realized the importance of "creative destruction." To establish the culture of a dynamic organization—and keep it growing—leaders need the courage to tear things apart and put them back together better than before. Greg is that kind of leader. He doesn't settle for the way things are. He's consistently willing to look at things from a new perspective, destroy the old, and rebuild with a refreshed vision. This shouldn't be a new concept for us. On the night Jesus was betrayed, He spent time with His closest followers. They may have been walking through a vineyard when He told them, "I am the true vine, and my Father is the gardener. He cuts off every branch in me that bears no fruit, while every branch that does bear fruit he prunes so that it will be even more fruitful" (John 15:1-2). Cutting off fruitful branches is creative destruction that produces much more fruit. More than any leader I know, Greg has the courage and creativity to make painful cuts that promise—and produce—much more growth.

Pain and suffering aren't the end of the world. I believe it's a foundational principle of life that discomfort is often the catalyst that forces us to discover new ideas, new methods, and new strategies of growth. I remember the board meeting when Greg told us he wanted to stop asking people for money. His idea was to put boxes in the room and let people take the initiative to put money there. I'm not the only person in the room who thought he had lost his mind! To my surprise, people were even more motivated to give generously when they didn't feel any pressure. (I guess Greg heard from the Lord and I'd had a bad burrito.)

It is my great privilege to recommend Greg and this book to you. God has used him in my life to refresh my vision more times than I can count. He is a gifted pastor, a bold leader, an insightful mentor, and even more, he is my friend.

TIM SCOTT
United States Senator from South Carolina

INTRODUCTION

One of my favorite things to do with pastors is to get them away from the busyness of their roles and invite them to join me and a few of their peers at a retreat. We may get together at a beach house near my home in Charleston, or we may go to a Crow Indian reservation in Montana. As we sit around the table at one of our first family-style meals, I ask the pastors to tell us the highs and lows they've experienced in the past year. They often talk about something God did in their own lives or in their families, such as a long hoped-for pregnancy, the return of a prodigal child, or a clean bill of health after a medical scare, but I tell them, "I know we don't want to compete with each other and talk about numbers at our churches, but this is a safe place. If one if your highs is a breakthrough at your church, tell us about it. Don't hold back!" I usually explain that when our church finally started to grow, I wanted to tell somebody—anybody!—but I wasn't sure who to tell. They laugh, but they get the point. They realize they have full permission to talk about the wonderful things God has done to answer prayer and propel their churches to another level of growth. Sometimes they tell the group about hiring a new staff person who has made a tremendous impact on the church, or that they had their highest attendance ever the past Easter.

AFTER A WHILE, IT'S A GRIND TO TRY TO MEASURE UP AND KNOW, WITH EACH FACEBOOK AND INSTAGRAM POST, THAT YOU'RE FALLING BEHIND.

After each person has talked about the highs, I ask them to be honest about the low points—difficult situations, and heartaches they've endured. In this kind of setting and with an invitation to be vulnerable, they find the courage to be brutally honest. Recently, in two groups of pastors at retreats I led, I listened for a long time as they poured out their hearts. Many were obviously struggling, even though they put on a positive face around their staff and the people in their churches. I could tell many of them felt overwhelmed and deeply discouraged. After a while I asked, "How many of you are on medications for anxiety and depression?" About half of the pastors in both groups raised their hands, and some that didn't raise their hands probably should have.

As I've listened to scores of pastors, I've realized that a lot of their discouragement comes from self-imposed, unrealistic expectations. Actually, they're not exactly self-imposed. They feel ashamed because they haven't hit the numbers others have listed in blogs and articles, and they can't face the shame of not measuring up. Comparison is eating their lunch! Social media has its value, but it can easily ruin your day. A pastor may be excited about baptizing six people, but when he sees that another pastor has baptized 2000 people on a single day, his elation falls off a cliff into the pit of despair. After a while, it's a grind to try to measure up and know, with each Facebook and Instagram post, that you're falling behind.

The biggest downer for a pastor of any size church is when people leave (and not because they're moving to a different city). Decades ago when we were starting Seacoast, if someone left the church, they often never said a word, or if they did, they wrote a letter to tell me about their decision. Today, some people don't go quietly; they post it online for the whole world to see! Oh, they try to be positive and say something like, "Our family went to such and such church today, and it was fantastic and life-giving! The teaching was the best I've ever heard, and the music inspired us! This is the right place for us. Hope to see you there next Sunday!" The responses are often from people at their previous church: "Oh, so you're not coming to our church anymore? Sounds like you found a great church!" How is the pastor of the church they left supposed to respond to posts like this? These words are like arrows piercing his soul. His anger is eclipsed only by the sadness of being perceived as "less than." Sometimes, staff members go to another church and post how wonderful it is at their new location... with the obvious negative comparison with where they've come from. This public shaming (that's what it is, whether it was meant to be or not) is a vision crusher.

When I meet with groups of pastors, I often ask, "What's a concern we can pray about while we're together?" Often, their chief worry revolves around money. Whether they are about to plant a church, or they lead large urban or suburban churches—financial problems know no limits. Recently, I was in a boat fishing with four guys, and as we fished, I discovered two of them didn't have health insurance for themselves or their families. These men lived with a looming cloud of enormous medical expenses they could encounter at any moment. Some pastors are trying to build great churches in parts of the country where housing and meeting space is exorbitantly expensive. Others are running up personal credit card debt to fund their churches until they become self-sustaining. Lord Jesus, come quickly!

Family problems are probably the most severe because they are most dear. These pastors suffer as they try to figure out how to help a child with a learning disability or a nagging medical problem. They may preach grace and power on Sunday mornings but wonder why God hasn't worked in the life of a prodigal son or daughter. Every moment of every day, they feel like they're failing the ones they love the most.

The strain of leading a church can easily wear on a marriage. Pastors have told me how they struggle with their spouses because the demands of the job take so much from them. I know exactly how they feel. Years ago, I set a lofty goal for Seacoast of having 2000 in attendance by the year 2000. On Easter Sunday in 1999, we hit that number. Later that afternoon as Debbie and I pulled into the driveway at our home, I was about to burst with excitement. I turned to her and said, "Did you know that we hit 2000 people today for the very first time?" She looked back at me without a hint of the elation I was feeling. She said bluntly, "That's your dream, not mine," and without another word, she got out of the car. At that moment, I realized Debbie and I had a problem, a big problem that wouldn't be fully resolved for two or three more years. The church, I reluctantly discovered, had become my mistress, and Debbie no longer felt cherished.

When I sit at a meal or in a boat with pastors and invite them to share the low points of their last year, at first they're understandably hesitant. They've seen what can happen when pastors are too self-disclosing, and they want to be careful to avoid saying too much too soon—and they certainly don't want to take the risk of being the only guy who's honest about a significant problem. I take the first step and share something that has been difficult for me, and soon, someone else takes the plunge. Before long, trust is built and people are more open than they thought they could ever be. They feel

Scott Hornsby, Billy Hornsby,
Chris Hodges, John Seibling and me
Duck Hunting - 2006

> *At any stage of a pastor's leadership and a church's development, vision can atrophy, passion can wane, and enthusiasm can vanish. From time to time, all of us need to have our vision refreshed.*

understood, and they feel valued. They can see that others have heard the worst about them and didn't laugh, offer a quick verse to fix their problem, or run away. Instead, they really listened.

At any stage of a pastor's leadership and a church's development, vision can atrophy, passion can wane, and enthusiasm can vanish. From time to time, all of us need to have our vision refreshed. Our circumstances may be very different from a pastor across town, and the stresses and pressures vary widely, but the effect is often very similar: the gradual erosion of the joy of seeing God use us to have an impact on people.

- You may be a church planter in your first three years when you wonder if your church is going to make it. That's enormous stress on a pastor and his family.

- You may have brought a fresh vision to a stagnant church, but the lethargy and resistance of the people are wearing you down.

- You may be the leader of a vibrant, growing church. Everything seems to be going exceptionally well, but you're emotionally, physically, and spiritually exhausted.

- You may have been blindsided by trouble you didn't see coming. Maybe it's a staff problem, maybe your board is resisting your leadership, or maybe you're having problems at home. Whatever it is, you feel deeply discouraged. The old solutions don't seem to be working, and you don't know where to turn.

Even the most successful leaders hit a wall at some point in their careers. They're successful only because they found a way to refresh their vision so they can keep moving forward.

If you're struggling and your vision for the future has become cloudy, know this: you're not alone. Others, including me, have walked where you walk. In this book, I want to rekindle your hope and give you some practical tools to help you move forward. Some problems have clear solutions and require only the courage to take the necessary steps. But most of the troubles we encounter have no crystal-clear answers. In those, we need to follow the processes God has given in His Word and listen to the advice of leaders who have been down this road before.

Each chapter of this book revolves around a piercing question that has shaped my journey as a pastor. I've wrestled with these questions, and I've seen God use them to stimulate reflection, clarify direction, and at least show me the first steps I needed to take. And as I've used these questions to launch discussions with other pastors, God has used them to bring wisdom and hope. I know what it's like to get up day after day and wonder if I'm walking in the path God has for me. I've second guessed myself a zillion times, and I've looked over my shoulder to see if anyone would follow me. We don't have to live with this kind of self-doubt, and worse, the shame of believing we don't have what it takes to be the leader God wants us to be. I trust God will use this book to give you hope and handles: hope for a better future and handles on the process of getting there.

At the end of this introduction and each chapter, you'll find some questions designed for personal reflection and perhaps a guide for discussions with your leadership team. I want to begin by asking you the same questions I've asked pastors on retreats. Don't rush through these. This isn't a timed test. Spend time prayerfully and patiently considering each one, and trust the Spirit of God to speak to you as you wade into them.

1

In the past year or so, what are the highs you've experienced? Consider your family, your walk with God, and your church's growth.

....

....

....

....

....

....

....

2

How did those successes and blessings fill your emotional tank and give you energy?

....

....

....

....

....

....

THINK ABOUT IT

3

What are the lows
you've endured?
(Write in code if you
need to.)

....
....
....
....
....
....
....
....
....
....
....
....
....
....
....
....
....
....
....
....
....

4

Did those struggles
erode (or shatter) your
vision for how God
would use you to build a
great church, or did you
find hope and strength
in the middle of them?
Explain your answer.

....
....
....
....
....
....
....
....
....
....
....
....
....
....
....
....
....
....
....

CHAPTER ONE

IF NOTHING
WERE IMPOSSIBLE

Q: WHAt ARE tHE Limits you Put On GOD AnD yOURSELF?

I am a dreamer—always have been, always will be. I've learned the hard way that dreams often go through cycles of birth, struggle, death, and resurrection. That's been my story. When I was a youth pastor, long before I ever thought of planting a church, Debbie gave me a little book titled *All Originality Makes a Dull Church* by Dan Baumann. The point of the book is that God is moving powerfully in existing churches, and we can learn important principles and practices from the leaders of these churches. In other words, pastors don't need to reinvent every facet of church structure, process, and worship to be successful. Baumann's book described the expansive vision and creative outreach of churches like Chuck Smith's Calvary Chapel, Gene Getz's Fellowship Bible Church, and Robert Schuller's Crystal Cathedral. My dreams suddenly got a lot bigger and much clearer as those pastors became a new model of leadership for me. I wanted to serve in a church like those...and someday be the pastor of a church like them.

Before I read this book, I perceived church as a place for believers with occasional forays into evangelism to bring outsiders to faith so they'd become insiders. The idea of the church doing effective (and culturally relevant) outreach in the community was new and exciting. In those years, I was a part-time volunteer youth pastor and a full-time employee of Hewlett-Packard in Ft. Collins, Colorado. A friend in the company was far from God. He was from a Catholic background, but it meant very little to him. He and his wife had a baby, but the child had severe medical problems. Within a month, their baby died. Debbie and I walked through the pain with them. We continued our friendship, and about a year later, he came to the church to meet with me. We were building a baptistry, and he asked, "What's that?" This question opened a wide-ranging conversation about God, and I was able to share the gospel of grace with him. He told me, "I think I'll start coming to church with you."

My immediate thought was, *Oh God, no!* Our church wasn't the kind of place where a person seeking God would feel comfortable and welcome. We talked often about reaching the nations, but we didn't have a clue about connecting in meaningful ways with our neighbors and friends. I was sure that if he came, it would be a disaster!

This conversation opened my eyes to see that I wanted to be a part of a very different kind of church, one where people like my friend would feel welcome...even *before* they trust Christ...and even if they *never* trust Christ. I wanted to build a church that attracted unchurched people instead of confusing them or repelling them. In a culturally relevant environment of love and truth, they could trust in the grace of Christ and experience His forgiveness, freedom, power, and direction. That was the beating heart of the dream God gave me. I had no concept of size. My vision was only the form and substance—the warmth of people reaching out to care for the people in their neighborhoods and at work, and seeing God do incredible things that only He can do.

About that time, Hewlett-Packard offered me a lot of money—salary, bonuses, benefits, and other perks—to move to Corvallis, Oregon, to open a new plant. It was an incredible offer, but in the same week, the pastor of the church where I had been the volunteer youth pastor asked me to come on their staff. He offered a salary of $6,500 a year, a small fraction of what I would make with Hewlett-Packard. The church had 250 to 300 people on Sundays. One of the stipulations of the offer, if I took it, was that Debbie couldn't work outside the home, so our income suddenly would have a concrete (and very low) cap on it.

I believed God wanted me to take the job with the church. Yes, it was crazy, but I was sure it was God's leading. Debbie and I had to make some drastic financial decisions. We had recently bought two cars, including a brand-new Toyota Celica, and we were living in a very nice apartment. All of that had to go. We sold our cars, bought a cheap one, and moved into low-income government housing (we qualified pretty quickly!) for $125 a month. I was the first staff member this pastor had ever had, and it was my first full-time church position. My role wasn't limited to leading the youth ministry. I was also the church secretary, the worship leader, and the assistant to the construction manager on the structure the church was building. I worked six days a week, Monday through Saturday. My day off was supposed to be Sunday, but I had a role in every meeting all day every Sunday, including leading a Sunday school class for the kids and participating in the Sunday night service. It didn't go well, and it didn't end well. He fired me within a year.

> I BELIEVED GOD WANTED ME TO TAKE THE JOB WITH THE CHURCH. YES, IT WAS CRAZY, BUT I WAS SURE IT WAS GOD'S LEADING.

Actually, this wasn't the first time I'd been fired. Let me tell some of the backstory: I went to college at Southwestern Assemblies of God University, and I was kicked out because I was a rock and roll guy. Then I went to Evangel College (now University) in Springfield, Missouri. I was the youth pastor at my Dad's church, and I took a couple of girls to a movie. In those days, this sin was considered just short of mass murder. Dad was furious. He told me, "Son, you can go to hell if you want to, but you're not going to corrupt the morals of the young people of this church! You're fired." I didn't know how I'd make up for the $5 a week he was paying me, but I'd try. After that, I went to Santa Monica, California, to serve at my grandfather's church. Soon after I arrived, the church fired my grandfather and me. (I'm not sure, but you may be able to detect a pattern here.)

Debbie and I moved to St. Louis, Missouri and lived in my parents' basement. My uncle was the District Secretary Treasurer of our denomination in the neighboring state of Illinois. I finally thought I knew what it would take to lead a vibrant, growing church, so I told my uncle I wanted to be a pastor. He said, "I can fix you up." He sent me as a candidate to a little church in a small town in the middle of the state. When I arrived, they had nine members. By this time, Debbie and I had been married for a couple of years, and we had a little baby. When we walked in, we increased the attendance by a third. Remarkable growth! That morning, I taught Sunday school and preached my heart out in the worship service. That afternoon, they voted. It was nine to nothing...against hiring me. Debbie and I drove back to my uncle's home. When I told him what happened, he didn't bat an eye. He immediately said, "No problem. I have another church for you in Freeport, Illinois." It was a much bigger church—13 members. He explained, "They'll vote, but it won't matter because this is a district-supervised church. You're in." I preached at their service, and they voted. This time it was 11 for me, none against, and two abstentions. I served at that church for over eight years, and it grew to about 400 people. (I always wondered who those two people were.)

Near the end of this time, the national and local economy took a nose-dive. Many people couldn't pay their mortgages, and they walked away from their homes. Our community had a 25 percent unemployment rate. We had been trying to build a larger building, but the interest rate was 18 percent. Our people were really struggling, and our family was no exception. By this point, Debbie and I had four small children. The truck for the WIC program (government sponsored resources for women, infants, and children) backed up to our church parsonage and unloaded milk, cereal, and other essentials every week. One day I got home and found Debbie crying. I asked her what was wrong, and she told me, "We're

DEBBIE & ME
- 1978 -

sending our kids to school without snow boots." I asked why she didn't buy boots for the children, and she looked at me the way wives look at husbands who really don't get it. She explained very carefully, "Because. We. Don't. Have. Any. Money."

After more than eight years in Freeport, the vision to create a different kind of church compelled me to make new plans. My uncle offered me a couple of larger churches in bigger cities, but I felt strongly that God wanted me to plant a church. He then agreed to back me, so I looked at three cities: Chicago, Houston, and Denver, where I grew up. For six months, I prayed and planned. I had recruited a team, and we were ready to go. Chicago, I was sure, was the place where God wanted us. I traveled there and planned to plant a church just across the highway from a new church called Willow Creek. I thought it might be a good idea for me to attend one of Willow's Sunday services. It was mind-blowing. One of the first people I saw was Mike Singletary, the All Pro linebacker for the Chicago Bears. And there were thousands of others in the service that day. After a few minutes, I realized it would be the better part of discretion to avoid competing with a church like that! However, my visit to Willow Creek wasn't a total bust. I had just attended the kind of church I had previously seen only in my dreams: one that understood what it means to welcome and love the unchurched.

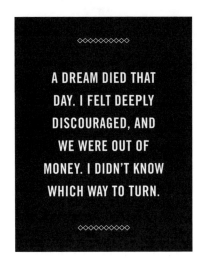

A DREAM DIED THAT DAY. I FELT DEEPLY DISCOURAGED, AND WE WERE OUT OF MONEY. I DIDN'T KNOW WHICH WAY TO TURN.

A dream died that day. I felt deeply discouraged, and we were out of money. I didn't know which way to turn. Seemingly out of the blue, Fred Richards, the pastor of Northwood Assembly in Charleston, South Carolina, called me. He said, "Greg, I don't know what you're doing right now, but our elders have been praying. We want to offer you a position on our staff as the head of our ministry to young adults. And by the way, we have a vision to plant churches someday...if you're interested in that."

We loaded up the truck and headed out from Freeport. Debbie and I cried during much of the trip. I'm sure the kids wondered where in the world we were taking them. I wondered, too. Northwood was a great church of about 1000 people—very balanced, loving, and strong. After three months in Charleston, I concluded that I wanted to be a staff member the rest of my life—much less pressure, no financial worries, and more time with my family. Life was good...very good.

One day Fred invited me to go to lunch with him. We had just ordered when he looked at me and said, "Greg, this isn't working."

I wanted to shout, "What do you mean it isn't working? It's the best situation I've ever been in!" But instead of words, I think my shock said everything I needed to say. Fred smiled and told me, "You're a number 1 guy, not a staff member. You need to be the pastor of your own church."

I had given up on that dream. The last eight years had been incredibly difficult, and I didn't know if I could put my family (and me) through that again. Fred leaned forward and said, "Greg, let's launch a church. That's your destiny."

The vision came alive again, but not without opposition. When I shared my idea of a church for the unchurched with some pastors and other leaders I

trusted, some of them said bluntly, "That's crazy. It'll never work." Their idea of radical, innovative leadership was to go to an existing church and help it grow, not start something new. But I was sure God wanted us to plant a church like Willow Creek to reach unchurched people.

The Northwood elders decided to launch the new church in Mt. Pleasant, a suburb of Charleston. Over several months, I put together a nucleus of about 55 people who were from that area and were driving into Charleston to church each week. Our strategy was to make phone calls to invite people to our first service. We asked them, "Are you attending a church?" If they said "yes," we told them, "That's great. Keep going there." If they said "no," we asked, "Why do you think most people don't go to church?" They usually said something about the music, or pastors too often asking for money, or distance, or time. No matter what they said, we invited them to come to our grand opening. Our team called every night for six weeks, and we reached over 16,000 homes. It was an uphill battle because in the weeks we were calling people, the news carried stories about the scandal at PTL and Jim and Tammy Faye Bakker, and then Jimmy Swaggart's sins were broadcast to the world. In this environment, unchurched people were understandably wary of Christian leaders. They had concluded that pastors are untrustworthy and only want your money. If people brought up these concerns, we asked, "If we address these issues, will you come?" Many said "yes."

We opened our doors on Easter Sunday, 1988, and we had 340 people show up. I was ecstatic! I called my best friend Terry Hilgers back in Denver and told him, "You've gotta come help me. Revival is breaking out! We might have 500 by the end of this month." I was sure there would be feature articles about us in leadership magazines within a few weeks. He quit his job and moved to Mt. Pleasant. By July, the South Carolina summer was steaming people like dumplings, and our church had about 160 people each week—less than half of the first week's attendance. A couple of months later, we were at 140.

I felt increasingly demoralized. I went back to the elders at Northwood Assembly three times and offered to resign, but they refused to accept my resignation. They told me, "This is all yours. Don't quit. We're with you." We continued to try to reach unchurched people, but we weren't growing. Images of Willow Creek tormented me. I felt like a colossal failure. We tried to use Willow Creek's dramas, but ours were horrible. (If you were in one or more of those and are offended, I'm sorry, but they were.) If you've ever had to

"You've gotta come help me. Revival is breaking out! We might have 500 by the end of this month."

preach after a disastrously bad drama, you know the anguish of trying to pull a clean sermon out of muddy drama pit. After three long years, we had plateaued at about 160 people.

A few people in our denomination looked on with measured skepticism. They had been sure that our ministry philosophy and worship style was a denial of the Holy Spirit. I had red marks all over me where I'd been poked so often by their 10-foot poles. The word I heard (or at least imagined) coming from their lips was "Ichabod!" Our ministry philosophy was simple: we provided wonderful, worshipful music as we reached out to unchurched people. It has become the model for many churches today, but back then, we were off to an unpromising start.

After five years, we finally got back to the number of people we'd had on that first Sunday: 340. I was excited (and greatly relieved). I had almost the same response I'd had years before. I thought revival was breaking out, and I had no idea what we'd do with all these people! One day, I went to the beach with my Bible, a Diet Coke, and a list of inspirational verses. Jesus told His disciples, "What is impossible with man is possible with God" (Luke 18:27). And He taught them to pray, "Your kingdom come, your will be done, on earth as it is in heaven" (Matthew 6:10). I thought, *Okay, this piece of earth is Mt. Pleasant, South Carolina. What if God's kingdom were to come to this community? What would it look like?* As I thought and prayed, a number came to mind: 2000. I thought, *It's 1993. Maybe we could reach 2000 people by the year 2000. Maybe that's what it means.* I was pretty squishy about what the word "reach" meant. I hoped it would be 2000 who had come to Christ and were attending our church, but I wasn't sure.

I drove home and opened my computer to a spreadsheet to figure out how much we had to grow each year to reach 2000 in seven years. It was about 25 percent each year. I drove to the library to look at census data for our part of the Charleston metro area: the number of people who are married, single, in each age bracket, income level, geographic distribution, and on and on. I found a study of a projection of income expected for a church based on attendance, and I factored in the staff ratios at each level of growth. Leadership expert Peter Wagner suggested one staff person per 100 in attendance, and to staff one person ahead, so two staff for 100 people, three for 200, and so on. I plugged all those numbers into the projections for each year before 2000. After I made these calculations, I made appointments to meet with local architects to find out how many square feet we would need for kids, students, classes, administration, and worship. I also met with school officials to ask how they planned best-use space for their students. I studied reports to discover how many visitors eventually became Christians and then members (or regular attenders). If we were going to grow by X number in a given year, we'd have to have Y number of visitors. All of this led to plans to attract those visitors and engage them. Let me list the questions that shaped the metrics of the progress I envisioned. At the risk of being redundant with some of them, it may help to put them in a list:

- What attracts new people? When and why do they come?

- How many first-time guests eventually become regular attenders?

- How many first-time guests will we need to hit our 25 percent growth rate each year?

- HOW MANY "COME AND SEE" MOMENTS DO WE NEED TO CREATE?

- HOW CAN WE GET OUR CURRENT MEMBERS TO INVITE THEIR FRIENDS?

- WHAT CAN WE DO TO INCREASE THE PROBABILITY VISITORS WILL COME BACK?

- HOW ARE WE GOING TO ASSIMILATE NEWCOMERS?

- HOW MANY SMALL GROUP LEADERS WILL WE NEED AT EACH STAGE OF GROWTH?

- HOW MANY SERVICES WILL WE NEED?

- HOW MANY STAFF MEMBERS WILL WE NEED EACH YEAR?

- HOW MUCH SPACE WILL WE NEED FOR EACH DEPARTMENT EACH YEAR?

- WHAT LEVEL OF FUNDING IS REQUIRED TO PROPEL GROWTH?

As I prayed through all this (and much more) and wrote on my spread-sheet, a familiar verse came to mind. The prophet Habakkuk heard from God: "The Lord answered me: 'Write down the vision; write it clearly on clay tablets so whoever reads it can run to tell others'" (Habakkuk 2:2 NCV).

I had never seen a strategic plan for a church, but instinctively, God led me to do the research to create one. I still have the notebook I created during this time. It's called "Vision 2000." I made no grand pronouncements of this goal—at least not yet. I didn't tell anyone at the church that this vision came from God. In fact, the only person I told was Debbie. I would follow God's command to Habakkuk when the right time came, but not too soon.

I had no context for this kind of growth. I'd only been in small churches until I came to Northwood, and I'd never seen any church grow rapidly. What would it take? I had no clue, but I trusted God to lead me. Tucked in the back of Paul's letter to the Colossians, he describes a man named Epaphras. He calls him "a servant of Christ Jesus" who "is always wrestling in prayer for you" and "is working hard for you" (Colossians 4:12-13). That's the pattern of leadership for all of us: to trust God with all our hearts and work like crazy to create moments in which the Holy Spirit works powerfully to transform lives. At Seacoast, we prayed, we followed the playbook, and we put in the sweat equity to build a church that God would use to build His kingdom on earth as it is in heaven.

> THAT'S the PATTERN OF LEADERSHIP FOR ALL OF US: to tRUST GOD with ALL OUR hEARTS AND WORK LIKE CRAZY to CREATE MOMENTS in which the HOLY SPIRIT WORKS POWERFULLY to tRANSFORM LIVES.

In 1999, a year early, we hit 2000 people at our church. Someone asked me, "Greg, why didn't you create this kind of plan before."

My answer was simple: "I'd never even thought of having one."

DREAM BIG

I'm astounded by what God has done in and through Seacoast. It's bigger and better than I ever imagined. Even with all my numbers, projections, and plans, God did more...much more. When I meet with pastors, I regularly ask them, "What would you attempt if you were ten times bolder? What would be the content and intensity of your prayers?"

Here's my advice: As you spend time letting God lead your thoughts to new ideas and a clearer vision, write it down...and keep writing as the vision is refined. Sooner or later, it needs to be simple and clear enough that you could text it while you're driving—but of course you'd never do that! Actually, you might have two statements, one for the people in your church and another for the church's numerical vision. For instance, many churches are using this purpose statement to shape the spiritual lives of their people:

KNOW GOD >>>>> FIND FREEDOM >>>>> DISCOVER PURPOSE >>>>> MAKE A DIFFERENCE

Your numeric goal can be as crisp and clear as the one I wrote in my journal on the beach that day in 1993: 2000 people by the year 2000. Yes, there are a million factors in the plan, but this simple statement captured my heart and gave me direction. I didn't feel comfortable sharing it with anyone but Debbie at first, and later, with our staff and board. Only much later did we tell the congregation about this audacious goal that would require the mighty power of God to accomplish it.

My story as a pastor is full of twists and turns, roadblocks and rapid acceleration. The path hasn't been smooth or linear. God has a way of humbling us and teaching us lessons through failure on the way to success. That's certainly my story, and it's very common among the pastors I know. So don't be surprised when your numbers decline for a while, when you pray but God doesn't seem to answer, when your family is less than thrilled at your bold vision, when people you counted on bail out, or when exhaustion causes you to second-guess yourself. Many young pastors assume that if they do what God told them to do, He'll smooth the way and they'll see dramatic and rapid growth. That's seldom the case. God often has a different agenda than our success. He takes the long view, and He uses setbacks, disappointments, and opposition to accomplish His purpose of preparing His shepherds to lead His people. The norm isn't a graph that's always "up and to the right"; the normal path for leaders is the death and resurrection of our dreams . . . and death is always really hard to take.

Through all the ups and downs of being a pastor, God has given me an anchor to keep me stable. In his letter to the Galatians, Paul encouraged them, "Let us not become weary in doing good, for at the proper time we will reap a harvest if we do not give up" (Galatians 6:9). That verse is so meaningful to me because I've thought about giving up dozens of times. Paul is showing us *we* have responsibilities and *God* has responsibilities.

- Our first responsibility is to learn how to *do good*, to study, to find great mentors, absorb leadership principles, and dive into the messy work of leading sheep. We can't control everything, but we control our commitment and intensity— what I call "the hustle factor." As we learn to do good, God will show us that our motives aren't always good and right and pure. That, too, is a valuable truth that enables us to live a life of repentance.

- The second responsibility for us is to *make doing good repeatable*. This means we create or adopt systems that facilitate others walking with God in effective ministry.

- Our third responsibility is to *avoid jumping ship*. I don't know of any leader who hasn't seriously considered quitting. Paul's simple and direct admonition is: "Don't do it!"

HERE'S THE OTHER SIDE OF THE EQUATION: GOD'S RESPONSIBILITY IS THE SIZE AND THE TIMING OF THE HARVEST.

Here's the other side of the equation: God's responsibility is the size and the timing of the harvest. We may think we can orchestrate growth, but we can't. Genuine spiritual growth is always the result of God's work in a person, a family, a church, and a community.

It's important to remember both sides of the equation: God controls the timing and the size of the harvest, and you control the hustle.

If we'll resign our perceived role as General Manager of the Universe, we can be sure that God already has the title and the power to make good happen. When we take too much responsibility and try to do God's job for Him, we create tremendous stress in us, we're difficult to live with, and we often get upset with God for not making our lives easier. We need to clearly understand the three responsibilities on our plates, and we need to reassign the responsibility for the harvest back to God.

My grandson Miles is a very talented soccer player. When he was ten, he scored five goals in a game, and of course, we were all thrilled. As I drove him to the next game, I asked, "Miles, how many goals are you going to score for Papa today?"

He thought for a few seconds and then said, "I'm going to score two for you today."

In the game, the coach put him on defense to counter the other team's best player. Miles' team won, but he didn't score any goals. When he came off the field, I told him, "Great game!"

He shook his head, "No it wasn't. I didn't score any goals today."

At that moment, the Holy Spirit opened my eyes. I told him, "Miles, I'll never again ask you how many goals you're going to score in a game. That's not fair because it puts too much pressure on you. I'll only ask you if you gave it all you have. You only have control over the hustle factor. That's your responsibility, not the number of goals."

Again, dream big, but know that it's God's job to produce the numbers in the seasons of your church. When you take responsibility for something only God can do — something that you have no authority over — you're hyper-charging your level of stress! Relax, trust God, and watch Him do what only He can do. Lead as if nothing is impossible with God...because that's the truth.

you only HAVE CONTROL OVER THE **HUSTLE** FACTOR.

MILES SURRATT WITH A CORNER KICK

THAT'S YOUR RESPONSIBILITY, NOT THE NUMBER OF GOALS.

THINK ABOUT IT

1

Describe the journey that has led you to this place today. What parts of it have been clear and positive, and what parts have been murky and difficult?

....

....

....

....

....

....

....

2

How would it help you to create a detailed, comprehensive plan for your church?

....

....

....

....

....

....

....

3

Does a plan like this
seem essential, or do
you think it takes God
out of the mix? Explain
your answer.

....

....

....

....

....

....

....

....

....

4

Describe the three
responsibilities on our
plates in Galatians 6:9.
What do (or would)
those look like in
your life?

....

....

....

....

....

....

....

....

....

5

Why is it crucial for your
spiritual and emotional
health to clearly
understand that God is
responsible for the size
and the timing of
the harvest?

....
....
....
....
....
....
....
....
....
....

6

What would you
attempt if you were ten
times bolder? What
would be the content
and intensity of
your prayers?

....
....
....
....
....
....
....
....
....

CHAPTER TWO

THE AIR WE BREATHE

Q: HOW CAN YOU CREATE A LIFE-GIVING CULTURE?

After I spoke at a conference, a sharp young pastor came up to ask a question: "Pastor Greg, what advice would your 60-year-old self give your 30-year-old self?" It was a brilliant question. When we started Seacoast, my ministry philosophy and strategy revolved around the vision God was giving me. I didn't give even a brief thought to the kind of culture that had to be crafted and nurtured to fulfill this vision. Today, my answer to the pastor's question is clear: I'd tell my 30-year-old self to spend much more energy creating a culture in which people thrive.

What makes a great organization? Why do some thrive, some strive, and some stagnate and die? Every good leader needs to birth and develop four essential organizational elements: vision, strategy, team, and culture. The *vision* tells people where the organization is going, the *strategy* describes how it will get there, the *team* determines who will bring their creativity and gifts so each person makes everyone else more effective, and the *culture* is the environment that stimulates people to achieve maximum success.

An organization's culture is the composite of unspoken assumptions, stated values, integrity, and cooperation. It affects every sphere of the organization's existence: the leadership team, all the staff, volunteers, those who attend, the neighborhood, and the entire community. The culture determines how success is celebrated, how failures crush people or help them grow, and whether the organization is ingrown or outward focused. The hours spent working or volunteering for the organization affects each individual's sense of purpose, family life, physical and mental health, and impact on others. The culture can unite or divide people of different races and backgrounds, promotes or destroys healthy relationships, and brings out the best in people or creates resentment and backstabbing.

Leaders can create environments in which every success is a stepping-stone and failure is never the last word about anybody's value. When we're secure enough to welcome input from people with different opinions, everybody wins. Historian Doris Kearns Goodwin has studied the presidents of the last couple of centuries, particularly Abraham Lincoln, Theodore Roosevelt, Franklin Roosevelt, and Lyndon Johnson. She observes, "Good leadership requires you to surround yourself with people of diverse perspectives who can disagree with you without fear of retaliation."

FOUR RESPONSIBILITIES

When a leader doesn't boldly and clearly establish the norms of the organization's culture, people either create their own (and compete with each other to spread their particular versions), try to guess (and often guess wrong), or give up and live in the wasteland of a flickering purpose. At Seacoast, we've defined four cultural responsibilities. Some churches use something similar as a purpose statement. It doesn't matter what you call it as long as your heart pumps it, and it runs through your veins. These four are:

1. love GOD with ALL OuR hEARts.

2. TREAt PEOPLE Right.

3. GEt BEttER.

4. mAintAin A gREAt AttituDE.

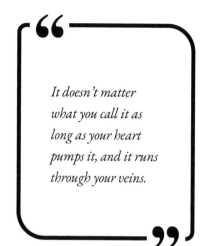

It doesn't matter what you call it as long as your heart pumps it, and it runs through your veins.

Culture is often exposed and formed in the furnace of difficulties. The full range of pressures uncover the true culture of a leader, a team, and an organization. Failure, or the threat of failure, creates doubts. The issue could be money, goals, expectations in performance, personal problems, or anything else. These are the times that shape and reinforce the "deep heart" of the organization. In such crucial times, people will remember what they felt in their relationships more than at any other time in the life of the organization.

1. LOVE GOD WITH ALL OUR HEARTS

The first and foremost responsibility is to focus on our relationship with God. A few years ago, I met with a man who leads a parachurch organization that provides wonderful resources for pastors. Somewhere during our conversation, I asked, "Tell me. Where do you go to church?"

He looked a bit sheepish, and after a few seconds, he said softly, "Well, my wife and I don't go anywhere anymore."

How does it happen that some of us who live to serve God can lose our desire to worship Him in community? We can become "professional Christians" and lose our passion for Jesus. Oh, we began our walks with God with the wonder of God's greatness and grace, and we couldn't get enough of His presence and power. Then we were introduced to the disciplines of Bible study, prayer, community, giving, and service, and those activities were fresh and transformative. At some point, we heard God's call to ministry, and we couldn't believe someone would pay us to pour our lives out for God. But somewhere along the way, we saw the "underbelly" of church life, and it wasn't pretty. Gradually, the thrill can ebb away, and we can "lose our first love"; and then, the ministry just becomes a job to earn a living. The wonder of knowing God and seeing Him use us deteriorates and something else takes its place: an imposing duty to fulfill the enormous expectations of those around us. We've traded glory for the grind.

A sense of awe is a non-negotiable for those of us in ministry. This tiny word has amazing power to promote happiness, peace, love, and physical health. Psychologists describe awe as the experience of encountering something so vast in size and beauty that our brains struggle to make sense of it. We are, quite literally, overwhelmed...in a positive way. It's the feeling of being touched by the beauty of art, nature, music, an unexpected kindness,

AWE IS THE MOST POWERFUL ANTIDOTE TO WORRY.

or the wonder of God's presence — experiences that are indescribable and leave us paradoxically feeling very small and yet very full.

Awe is the most powerful antidote to worry. In an article for *Inc.*, clinical psychologist Robert Leahy explains, "When anxiety strikes, its sufferers are overwhelmed by, and hyper-focused on, their own worrisome, dark thoughts. It's a state that infuses an often misleading sense of 'realness' or 'correctness' to those thoughts." In other words, worry makes us think the worst is absolutely true and failure is inevitable! Leahy continues, "Rumination — or mulling over worries — is the biggest predictor of depression and anxiety." In the article, another expert, Carlin Flora, asserts that awe-inspiring experiences "ignite intellectual curiosity and provide aesthetic pleasures, but they also pull us out of our default mode of self-absorption."[1] A study published in the *Journal of Personality and Social Psychology* discovered that inducing a sense of awe supports ethical decision making, increases generosity, and stimulates productive social interactions—it makes people nicer.[2] Awe makes you a better leader and a better person.

---

1 "For Less Stress, Try More Awe," Jessica Stillman, *Inc.*, March 16, 2016, https://www.inc.com/jessica-stillman/the-missing-ingredient-for-greater-psychological-health-awe.html

2 Cited by American Psychological Association, "Awe may promote altruistic behavior," May 19, 2015, https://www.sciencedaily.com/releases/2015/05/150519091132.htm

We can't manufacture awe like we produce a ministry plan or conference schedule, but we can take three definitive steps to rekindle it and inspire it.

*** REMEMBER ***

First, remember times when the wonder of God was palpable to you. You saw, felt, and sensed the presence of God around you, in you, and working through you to touch the lives of others. This is an easy one for me. People sometimes ask, "Did you always want to be a pastor?" The answer is "no." I wanted to play in a band and be a rock star. Along with some other guys, we formed a pretty good band. In fact, one of us, Brent Rowan, became a world-renowned guitar player. He has played on songs that have sold over 100 million albums. Brent and I grew up in a little church, and our parents wouldn't let us listen to rock and roll, but we found a way to not only listen but to make music. The day after we graduated from high school, we went to Chicago to play four nights a week for six weeks. As we rehearsed before the last night, one of the guys said, "I think we need to say something about Jesus when we finish."

"Like what?" I asked.

"I don't know," he smiled. "You'll think of something."

"Me?"

"Yeah, your dad's a pastor. You can do it."

At that time, I was following Jesus...from a distance. I had no desire to say-anything to the people who were going to come that night, but under coercion, I reluctantly agreed to give it a shot.

We finished playing in front of almost a thousand young people, and before we left the stage, I opened my mouth and told them about the love of Jesus. I don't know who was more surprised, the kids in the crowd, the guys in the band, or me. It was an out-of-body experience. I made an appeal for people to respond to the gospel...and a few hundred came forward! I felt transported, maybe not to the third heaven like the Apostle Paul, but to somewhere I'd certainly never been before. Years later, I found out that some of the kids who came to the stage to receive Christ are now pastors, and some had been gang members who found hope, forgiveness, and a new purpose that night. The next day I called my girlfriend (who later became my wife) to tell her what happened. To that point, she had been thinking about marriage, but I had a one-track focus on rock music and our band. But in that call, I said, "You know all those plans I've been making? I may not become a rock star after all. I don't know, but I might become a, uh, a preacher or something." The experience with God that night was amazing...stunning...transforming...and I when I remember it today, I'm still genuinely full of wonder.

A few years ago, I asked Brent to come to Seacoast and play for us. He and I played "Amazing Grace," and then I asked him some questions. I said, "Brent, people know I play the guitar...just like you. But they want to know just how good I was back in the day when we had our band. Would you tell them?"

With all the stage presence of a gifted performer, Brent looked at the crowd and told them, "Well Greg, it's like this: in Nashville, there are two types of musicians, those with talent and those with instruments. You had instruments." I guess following the Lord's call to be a pastor wasn't really at the cost of not being on the cover of *Rolling Stone*.

I've noticed that almost anything can erode our sense of awe. When we're successful, we can conclude it's because of our magnetic personality and magnificent talents, and our attitude drifts from gratitude to entitlement. When we fail, we may think God has forgotten us, that He hasn't fulfilled His promises of blessings, and we tumble into the pit of self-pity. And when we're exhausted, always busy and under the gun of other's demands, the joy of serving God and loving others seems like a distant memory. Don't let the necessity of cultivating a sense of awe get pushed aside. It's essential if we're going to make it as leaders.

*** Write An inventory ***

The second recommendation to rekindle wonder is to take time to write a personal inventory of people, things, opportunities, and experiences you're thankful for. Make this about your current condition, not the past. Scrape away the entitlement, the resentments, and the self-pity, and dig deep into the heart of God to consider all He is to you, all He has given you, and all He is doing through you. If this seems like a struggle, try to think of 10 blessings you've received from God, and tomorrow, ask God to open your mind and heart to 10 more, and do the same thing for the next few days. There's no hurry and no contest for the most on a list. Let this exercise awaken your gratitude so that it pushes out (or at least begins to push out) the anxiety that weights you down.

*** Give thAnks ***

Third, now that you've remembered and written your inventory, take time to reflect on all this and pour out your heart in thanksgiving to God for letting you be in this place at this time with these people for this season.

You might ask, "What do these three things have to do with the cultural responsibility to love God?" My answer is, "Everything!" We love because He first loved us. God is the initiator, the prime mover, the pursuing lover who wanted us as His own before the foundations of the world were laid. We deserve nothing, but He has given us everything pertaining to life and godliness. The experience of His grace humbles us to the dust because we realize we're not worthy, but then it affirms us to the skies because we're amazed that the God of the universe gave himself for us! That's where we began when we first trusted in Christ, and that's where we stay as we go deeper and deeper into the bottomless well of His love, forgiveness, acceptance, kindness, and power. We drift away from Him at our peril, but we have His assurance that He always warmly welcomes us back. This assurance, this sense of awe, is our fountain of joy and our foundation of strength as we trust God to use us to create a vibrant culture.

2. TREAT PEOPLE RIGHT

The second responsibility is to treat people with respect and love. Virtually every one of the world's great religions has some version of the Golden Rule: Treat others the way you want to be treated. It's not that hard to understand, but from looking at the news each night and talking to people in our communities, it appears that this simple directive is rarely lived out.

When we consider how to respond to a spouse, a child, a staff member, a volunteer, a person in the congregation, or a sales clerk at the store, it takes only a little effort to try to see the situation from the other person's point of view. We can ask ourselves, *What's going on with that person? What does he (or she) need from me right now?* Paul wrote the Colossians that treating people right comes from a heart that has been melted and molded by the grace of God. Only when our hearts are filled and overflowing with God's love will we give, forgive, love, and serve with no strings attached. Paul explained:

> Therefore, as God's chosen people, holy and dearly loved, clothe yourselves with compassion, kindness, humility, gentleness and patience. Bear with each other and forgive one another if any of you has a grievance against someone. Forgive as the Lord forgave you. And over all these virtues put on love, which binds them all together in perfect unity. (Colossians 3:12–14)

When we treat people this way, we form a spiritual family, one that heals instead of hurts, builds instead of bludgeons, and inspires instead of ignores. Paul wrote to his young protégé Timothy about the nuances of relating to each age group in his church: "Do not rebuke an older man harshly, but exhort him as if he were your father. Treat younger men as brothers, older women as mothers, and younger women as sisters, with absolute purity" (1 Timothy 5:1-2). This takes the Golden Rule into the church to turn us into a strong, loving, supportive family. The church is a body, not a business. Sure,

> *Only when our hearts are filled and overflowing with God's love will we give, forgive, love, and serve with no strings attached.*

we need to run it with good management and financial skills, and a family needs to use the same skills to operate effectively—but a family needs much more than administrative skills.

Kindness is the oil that makes the machine of life run more smoothly, and it affects even those who aren't the direct givers or recipients. A Dartmouth study found, "The positive effects of kindness are experienced in the brain of everyone who witnessed the act, improving their mood and making them significantly more likely to 'pay it forward.' This means one good deed in a crowded area can create a domino effect and improve the day of dozens of people!" The study discovered that observing acts of kindness releases oxytocin, the "love hormone," lowering blood pressure and anxiety and increasing a sense of optimism. In fact, kindness stimulates another chemical in the brain, serotonin, which produces a sense of peace, calm, and happiness. The study concludes, "Perpetually kind people have 23% less cortisol (the stress hormone) and age slower than the average population!"[3]

Leaders aren't too busy or too important to be kind to the people around them. We might be tempted to excuse our brusque, demanding behavior because we're convinced we have "a higher calling" and "we're under so much pressure," but our first calling is to respond to Jesus' summons: "Follow Me." As we examine the life of Jesus, we find Him incredibly and consistently kind to the people He encountered—including the dense disciples. Yes, He was strong and defiant with the religious leaders, but primarily to confront them for their lack of compassion for the sick, the blind, the lame, women, children, and the poor. What stirred up His anger most frequently? The lack of kindness among those leaders!

---

3   "Kindness Health Facts," Dartmouth Edu, https://www.dartmouth.edu/wellness/emotional/rakhealthfacts.pdf

No matter how busy we are, one of our priorities is to make the people around us feel valued and loved. Let me offer three very practical ways we can show kindness to others.

1. Be quick to forgive their past sins and failures.

2. Believe the best about their motives and contributions in the present.

3. Speak prophetically into their future.

Giving words of hope and vision is one of our most important roles as leaders. It takes time to think and pray about what we see around the corner for the people we lead, but it means the world to them when we put words on their highest (but often poorly defined) hopes for the future. Jesus told the big fisherman, "Simon, you were this, but Peter, you will be that." I can imagine this single statement resonated with him throughout the rest of his life, especially in the dark days after he betrayed Jesus. Zacchaeus had been a short, greedy crook, but Jesus pronounced that he had been radically transformed into a generous and gracious follower. Do you think Zacchaeus thought of this pronouncement in the coming months and years? You bet he did!

3. GET BETTER

Third, we make a commitment to continually improve. I'm not referring to talents or gifts; I'm talking about our dedication to do a great job in whatever role we play. This is the "hustle factor." We can't control the harvest, but we can control the hustle—our investment of energy and intensity. This commitment starts at the top and permeates the team and all volunteers. This has nothing to do with titles or power. Everyone can be devoted to getting better. Martin Luther King, Jr. famously preached, "If a man is called to be a streetsweeper, he should sweep streets even as Michelangelo painted, or Beethoven composed music, or Shakespeare wrote poetry. He should sweep streets so well that all the hosts of heaven and earth will pause to say, here lived a great streetsweeper who did his job well."[4] Excellence is everyone's calling.

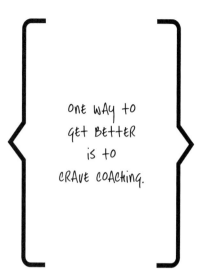

One way to get better is to crave coaching.

After I preached my heart out for a little church in Illinois and they voted nine to nothing not to hire me, I was very discouraged. (Debbie was thrilled. She didn't want to go there.) That night, we drove back to Carlinville, Illinois, where my grandparents lived. They could tell my confidence had been shattered that day, so they suggested we drive to Springfield, Missouri, to hear M.C. Johnson at Calvary Assembly. When we walked in, I saw almost a thousand people. I thought, Someday, maybe...Later, I had the opportunity to ask Pastor Johnson some questions about success in ministry. Among the many insights he gave me, he said, "If you are leading a meeting, every minute past one hour early is late." He could tell I was a bit surprised, so he explained that he had seen too many pastors far too often run into a meeting unprepared and frantic to figure out how to lead it. Being ready and fully prepared isn't a luxury; it's a necessity.

---

4   Martin Luther King, Jr., "The Three Dimensions of a Complete Life," New Covenant Baptist Church, Chicago, Illinois, April 9, 1967, https://kinginstitute.stanford.edu/king-papers/publications/knock-midnight-inspiration-great-sermons-reverend-martin-luther-king-jr-6

One way to get better is to crave coaching. A few years ago, I had the opportunity to speak at the chapel for the Indianapolis Colts football team. They were playing my favorite team, the Denver Broncos, and their former quarterback, Peyton Manning was making his first return to Indianapolis as the quarterback for the Broncos. Apparently, I did much too good a job with the chapel because the Colts won the game...much to my chagrin.

My friend, Clyde Christenson, was the quarterbacks coach for the Colts, and I had a chance to ask him a lot of questions about the Colts culture. One story stuck out in particular. Every year at the team's preseason workouts, All Pro receiver Reggie Wayne told the coaching staff to "coach me like a rookie." You would assume that a player of his status would get a few perks that rookies don't get, like lighter workouts and preferential treatment. Not Reggie. He recognized that even All Pros need to make improvements.

No matter how far we've come as leaders, we need to remember that we can't get better without accurate feedback, and we almost certainly won't get accurate feedback if we don't crave coaching.

Another way to get better is to learn from people who know more than you. There is always someone a few steps ahead of where you are in your journey. Most would be honored to share their knowledge. The right questions can often open the door to valuable insight.

We ask each member of our team to find at least three people somewhere in the world who seem to be doing their job better and learn from them. Texts, phone calls, in-house visits can all push us toward the value of getting better. Excellence isn't a skill; it's an attitude. When we understand this principle, we're open to the input of others, not ashamed that everything

COLTS VS. BRONCOS 2013

COACH CLYDE CHRISTENSON AND ME

isn't perfect. We ask other pastors, our staff members, and even volunteers for input...and we genuinely listen. We borrow their eyes because they often see things we never noticed—not only the flaws but also the blessings and opportunities. There's a story of a military general who, when a courier came with information from the battlefield, regularly asked the private or corporal, "Young man, what do you think we should do?" He didn't always take the courier's advice, but he realized a person who had been in the thick of the fight on another part of the battlefield just might have a valuable suggestion.

Over the years, I've learned to be a student of other leaders' perceptions. When they see things I missed, I asked, "How did you notice that? Tell me more about what you see." I'm intentionally borrowing their eyes.

4. MAINTAIN A GREAT ATTITUDE

And fourth, infectious optimism needs to be cultivated and celebrated. No matter how many resources a church has acquired, no matter how talented the staff may be, no matter the size of the church, a pervasively bad attitude poisons the culture. I'm not suggesting everyone should sit around singing "Kumbaya." Show me an organization without significant stress, and I'll show you one that's getting nothing done. Show me an organization that has no personality conflicts, and I'll show you an organization with one employee. Show me an organization that has perfectly equal treatment of all people, and I'll show you a cemetery. Stress and conflict are inevitable in a growing, healthy collection of humans, whether it's in a marriage, with kids, a business, a small group, and in any size church. Until we are in boxes in the ground, deadlines will keep coming, people will disappoint us, and the unexpected will pop up. If we think we should be immune from all of this, we'll be continually surprised and angry. We'll sabotage our joy, and we'll block the creative juices needed to address these problems. Entitlement inevitably leads to a sullen attitude, and this attitude is as contagious as Ebola.

We've all heard it, and we've all said it, but it's true: a leader's job is to be a thermostat, not a thermometer: a thermometer reflects the temperature of the room, but the thermostat sets the temperature. Similarly, our attitude sets the temperature of the room, and every person is affected. And the thermostat needs to be the same in private and in public. Too many pastors are praised for their platform skills but are bears in their interactions with people on their teams. Our attitude in staff meetings, at home, and in private meetings needs to reflect the love, power, and purpose we preach from the pulpit. If not, the people closest to us—our spouses, kids, and staff members—will see us as phony, and this observation kills the culture of an organization.

Of course, as we're open and honest, we need wisdom to be sure we don't share information that isn't appropriate, either on the stage, in staff meetings, or one-on-one. This doesn't mean we have permission to have a secret life. We need at least one person who knows our deepest secrets, and we need to be wisely vulnerable with each group we lead. Vulnerability about heartaches and struggles needs to be combined with a strong commitment to trust God for His answers in His timing. Truth and grace—that's what Jesus brings to the world and to each of us, so we can be honest and hopeful at the same time.

Solomon, the wisest man the world has known (except for Jesus, of course), gave this supreme advice to his son: "Above all else, guard your heart, for everything you do flows from it" (Proverbs 4:23). We guard our hearts by observing our attitudes, words, and actions, and when we're running off the rails, we need to take corrective action. That doesn't mean just shutting up (which may, in fact, be entirely appropriate); it also means going back to the wonder of God's grace, trusting in His omniscience and omnipotence, and believing that He hasn't given up on our future. We guard our hearts by keeping them centered on the love, wisdom, timing, and power of God. I've learned that when times are tough, we need to go deeper into God's grace, be tenaciously thankful, trust God for the harvest, and pay kindness forward.

Our attitudes don't have to be dictated by our circumstances. We're usually positive when things are going well and grumpy when they aren't, but there's another way. When we rivet our hearts on the greatness and grace of God, we unleash the power of God into the messes of our lives.

Paul and Silas had followed God's call to take the gospel to Europe. At Philippi, they led Lydia to Christ and cast a demon out of a slave girl. Things were going well at that point, but the girl's owners grabbed the two men and dragged them before the magistrates, accusing them of "throwing [the] city into an uproar." At that point, a crowd attacked them, and the magistrates ordered them to be stripped and beaten. When they were bloody pulps, they were thrown into the deepest part of a prison and put in stocks. At that point, most of us would seriously question whether we'd heard God clearly when He told us to go there! But Paul and Silas trusted that God was in control and somehow would use their predicament to advance the kingdom.

> *When we rivet our hearts on the greatness and grace of God, we unleash the power of God into the messes of our lives.*

At midnight, they sang hymns. (I can imagine the pain they felt as they sang, but it didn't stop them.) God caused an earthquake, the cell doors swung open and their chains fell off. The jailer was about to commit suicide, which was the appropriate response to his failure to keep the prisoners in jail, but Paul stopped him. Paul led the jailer and his family to Christ. The fledgling church in Philippi began with a rich lady who was a fabric merchant, a slave girl, and a jailer and his family. Think about the stories they could tell visitors to the church! (See Acts 16:16–40.)

A few years later, when Paul wrote to the church in Philippi from a Roman jail, he explained that his present imprisonment wasn't outside of God's plan. In fact, it was squarely in God's sovereign design:

> Now I want you to know, brothers, that what has happened to me has really served to advance the gospel. As a result, it has become clear throughout the whole palace guard and to everyone else that I am in chains for Christ. Because of my chains, most of the brothers in the Lord have been encouraged to speak the word of God more courageously and fearlessly. (Philippians 1:12–14)

In both jails, Philippi and Rome, Paul didn't complain, he didn't give up on God, and he didn't give up on God's purpose for him. He had a much bigger picture of God and His purposes than his present condition. He was convinced that a loving God is redeeming mankind from the consequences of sin, and He'll use every circumstance to accomplish this purpose...if we'll trust Him. The big picture is God bringing the gospel to the world, and somehow, our current condition is part of the richly textured fabric of His purposes. When we forget that truth, we grumble. What does it take for us to slip into a bad attitude?

To develop and keep a good attitude, we need to focus on the right things. I'm an amateur photographer, and I've learned (the hard way) that it's crucial to focus the lens on the right subject. I've taken too many pictures of sharply focused doors and lamps and very fuzzy people in front of them. When this happens, the important things are out of focus and the trivial are the center of attention. That's a metaphor of how easy it is to lose our focus and develop a bad attitude. When we spend far too much time on the trivial things, the most important truths about God, about ourselves, and about God's plan for us become blurry. Even in prison, Paul didn't lose sight of what's most important. In the same passage in his letter to the Philippians, he assured them,

> It is true that some preach Christ out of envy and rivalry, but others out of goodwill. The latter do so out of love, knowing that I am put here for the defense of the gospel. The former preach Christ out of selfish ambition, not sincerely, supposing that they can stir up trouble for me while I am in chains. But what does it matter? The important thing is that in every way, whether from false motives or true, Christ is preached. And because of this I rejoice. Yes, and I will continue to rejoice. (Philippians 1:15–18)

Paul was in prison, and his reputation was being torched by jealous Christians, but he didn't care. All that mattered to him was that the gospel was getting out to more people. Paul let his readers know that they played an important role in fulfilling God's purposes:

> . . . for I know that through your prayers and God's provision of the Spirit of Jesus Christ what has happened to me will turn out for my deliverance. I eagerly expect and hope that I will in no way be ashamed, but will have sufficient courage so that now as always Christ will be exalted in my body,

whether by life or by death. For to me, to live is Christ and to die is gain. (Philippians 1:19–21)

Paul's attitude gave him an inclusive perspective about how God uses other people. Most pastors are fiercely competitive. We don't want to admit it, but we are. One pastor said that he went to a pastors' conference, and immediately, people were sizing each other up to see where they were on the pecking order of the size of their churches. We often turn up our noses at leaders of other denominations and faith traditions, and we look for things that we disagree with so we can feel superior. But Paul didn't do that at all. He looked past the motives of the evangelists who wanted to take his place, and he rejoiced that more people were hearing about Jesus.

So to get and keep a good attitude, get God's perspective, then focus on what's really important, and finally, remember your mission. In the same passage, Paul continued:

> If I am to go on living in the body, this will mean fruitful labor for me. Yet what shall I choose? I do not know! I am torn between the two: I desire to depart and be with Christ, which is better by far; but it is more necessary for you that I remain in the body. Convinced of this, I know that I will remain, and I will continue with all of you for your progress and joy in the faith, so that through my being with you again your boasting in Christ Jesus will abound on account of me. (Philippians 1:22–26)

Paul was torn between two desires: to leave and be with Christ or to stay and serve Christ. Either way, it was all about Christ. The question Paul inherently asks us is this: "Why aren't you dead yet?" God leaves us on earth for a purpose, not to make money or acquire fame or experience pleasure,

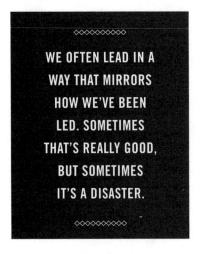

WE OFTEN LEAD IN A WAY THAT MIRRORS HOW WE'VE BEEN LED. SOMETIMES THAT'S REALLY GOOD, BUT SOMETIMES IT'S A DISASTER.

though He may give these in some measure. He leaves us here for the benefit of other people. We are servants first of God and then of the people He puts in our path each day. God has given us the unspeakable privilege of being His hands, His feet, and His voice to care for people in need, inspire those who are growing, and communicate the transforming message of grace to everyone. That's why God left Paul on earth, and that's why He lets us hang around, too.

When we have this perspective, joys are multiplied and we have a very different expectation of God's purposes for our struggles. They're never a shock to God. No matter what the cause, even if it's because we've sinned and we're experiencing the consequences, every moment in our lives will be drenched in God's redemptive purposes if we'll believe in His grace and be open to His leading. No matter what's happened, God always has a much bigger purpose than we can ever imagine. Count on it. It's true.

BEING INTENTIONAL

Many leaders take culture for granted. They shouldn't. We often lead in a way that mirrors how we've been led. Sometimes that's really good, but sometimes it's a disaster. We need to be students of our own leadership style so we can assess the kind of culture we're creating. Some would assume this analysis is always subjective, but there are some important elements we can see and measure, for instance:

JOSH SURRATT AND CHURCH PLANTERS IN SWITZERLAND

- How much churn do you have in your staff and top volunteers? A high turnover rate probably reflects the fact that people don't feel comfortable and fulfilled. They may be reacting to too much control or too little direction, harsh communication or feeling ignored. Pay attention, and don't assume "it's on them."

- If fear and intimidation are the primary motivators, you've got a lousy culture. How can you tell if this is the motivation of even some of the people you lead?

- Do people laugh easily and enjoy being together? Or is the laughter laced with sarcasm?

- Do people feel comfortable disagreeing with you and each other, or are they afraid to voice their ideas and concerns?

- Listen to third-person evaluations of your team and your church. In other words, what are people saying to each other about you and the atmosphere of the church?

- Are people lined up to join your team, or is it hard to fill slots?

- How much fun do you and your people have together?

Chip Judd, one of our staff at Seacoast, uses a term that perfectly describes a healthy culture. He says that a team that loves, supports, and stimulates each other "lives well." This quality is pervasive and transferable, that is, this kind of environment affects everyone at every level of the church, and it works in urban, suburban, and rural settings.

Healthy cultures don't just happen. They are the product of an intentional, prayerful plan and a patient process to create relationships that bring out the best in each person. Paul described this kind of culture in his letter to the Romans: "Love must be sincere. Hate what is evil; cling to what is good. Be devoted to one another in love. Honor one another above yourselves. Never be lacking in zeal, but keep your spiritual fervor, serving the Lord. Be joyful in hope, patient in affliction, faithful in prayer" (Romans 12:9–12).

Principles about creating a healthy culture didn't come instinctively to me. I had to learn them over many years. I wish someone would have taught them to my 30-year-old self, but I'm not sure I would have listened. Today, I see the formation of a vibrant culture as one of the chief responsibilities of leaders. It can't be delegated, and it can't be ignored. Paul demonstrated a godly perspective and a faith-filled attitude when he experienced the greatest pain, the deepest darkness, and the biggest heartache because Christian leaders were thrilled he was in prison. That's our story too: we learn the value of crafting a healthy culture during times of doubt, suffering, and setbacks. As we learn them and apply the principles, we'll be free from the grip of comparison, we'll experience more hope that God will work in every circumstance, and our people will have a leader worth following.

HEALTHY CULTURES
DON'T JUST HAPPEN.

↓ ↓ ↓

THEY ARE THE
PRODUCT OF AN
INTENTIONAL
&
PRAYERFUL
PLAN.

THINK ABOUT IT

1

How would you describe a toxic church culture, one that is doing only okay, and one that's healthy?

....
....
....
....
....
....
....

2

Why is a sense of awe so important, and, in fact, a top priority, for leaders?

....
....
....
....
....
....
....

3

What are some practices
you use to rekindle
your wonder at God's
greatness and grace?

....
....
....
....
....
....
....
....
....

4

Take some time, today
and over the next few
days, to remember
moments in the past
when you had a sense of
wonder at the greatness
and grace of God...write
down an inventory of
what God has done for
you, in you, and through
you...and pour out your
heart in gratitude
to Him.

....
....
....
....
....
....
....
....
....
....

5

Who has been especially
kind to you? How did
that person affect you?

....

....

....

....

....

....

....

....

....

....

....

....

....

....

....

....

....

....

....

....

6

How much do you crave
coaching? Who is, or
could become,
your coach?

....

....

....

....

....

....

....

....

....

....

....

....

....

....

....

....

....

....

....

....

7

What do we learn from
Paul's experience in the
Philippian jail and the
insights in his letter to
the church there?

....

....

....

....

....

....

....

....

....

....

....

....

....

....

....

....

....

....

....

8

How would you answer
the questions under
"Being Intentional"?

....
....
....
....
....
....
....
....
....
....
....
....
....
....
....
....
....
....
....
....
....

9

What are two or three
specific steps you can
take to create a healthier
culture in your church?

....

....

....

....

....

....

....

....

....

....

....

....

....

....

....

....

....

....

....

CHAPTER THREE

PRODDED BY THORNS

Q: HOW CAN CURRENT LIMITATIONS BE USED AS A CATALYST FOR GROWTH?

Some leadership gurus try to stimulate an expansive vision by asking, "What would you do if you had no limits?" I'm sure this question may be helpful in some ways, but the truth is that we all have limitations. Even Superman was limited by Kryptonite!

In one of the most enigmatic statements in the Scriptures, Paul tells us that Jesus "emptied himself." What does that mean? Surely, He didn't empty himself of His deity, but when He was in human form, He was at least no longer omnipresent for that time, and we get only fleeting glimpses of His glory, like on the Mount of Transfiguration and after the resurrection. In contrast, our limitations don't need much deep theological study—they're readily apparent! We are limited in our finances, talents, wisdom, location, opportunities, and time, to name a few. We live within a paradox: nothing is impossible with God, but we have to cope with very real limitations.

Paul shares his perspective on the limits he faced:

> Therefore, in order to keep me from becoming conceited, I was given a thorn in my flesh, a messenger of Satan, to torment me. Three times I pleaded with the Lord to take it away from me. But he said to me, "My grace is sufficient for you, for my power is made perfect in weakness." Therefore I will boast all the more gladly about my weaknesses, so that Christ's power may rest on me. That is why, for Christ's sake, I delight in weaknesses, in insults, in hardships, in persecutions, in difficulties. For when I am weak, then I am strong. (2 Corinthians 12:7–10)

Paul had amazing talents. He was a brilliant thinker and one of the world's most gifted leaders. From one point of view, he had every reason to be arrogant and self-sufficient, but he wasn't. God allowed Satan to torment him for a specific purpose. Paul prayed three times for relief, but no relief came. Instead, God gave him a new perspective on his thorny limitation: in the limitation, God would show His grace and power more fully than ever before. Paul's limitation would be a channel of even more spiritual depth and vitality. Paul learned the lesson. He concluded that his very limitations were the stage for God to display His mighty power. With that concept woven deep in his heart, Paul could actually delight in his limits because only then could he experience more of God.

If Paul were preaching to us about this passage, I think he'd include these important points:

- Limitations — everybody's got 'em.

- God gives them (or allows them) for a purpose — in this case, to keep him humble. Whatever other purposes God has for our deficiencies, we can conclude that all limitations are designed to deepen our dependence on God. They are standard operating procedure in God's discipleship plan for every believer.

- There's nothing wrong with asking God to take the limitations away, but the answer may be "no." God didn't blame Paul for not having enough faith and for that reason refuse to answer his prayers. No, God had a different curriculum for Paul . . . and often, for us.

- We can either whine about our limitations or see them from God's perspective and rejoice in them. (This goes back to the point in the previous chapter about keeping the most important things in focus and letting the trivial things fade into the background. The problem, of course, is that in times of trouble, it's hard to conclude that the very evident pain is trivial and God's unseen purposes are far more important.)

"Do you think I missed God's calling? Is that why things aren't going well?"

- If we trust Him, God will display His power in us and through us because of, not in spite of, our limitations.

Far too often, we draw the wrong conclusion when things don't work out the way we planned. Pastors who have endured setbacks or long periods of meager growth in their ministries have asked me, "Do you think I missed God's calling? Is that why things aren't going well?"

I usually tell them, "No, not necessarily at all. Your difficulties may well be God's classroom where you can learn valuable lessons you'll need for the rest of your life. Don't miss them!" When God told Moses to lead the people out of Egypt, He didn't give him the full picture at first. God told him,

> "I have indeed seen the misery of my people in Egypt. I have heard them crying out because of their slave drivers, and I am concerned about their suffering. So I have come down to rescue them from the hand of the Egyptians and to bring them up out of that land into a good and spacious land, a land flowing with milk and honey—the home of the Canaanites, Hittites, Amorites, Perizzites, Hivites and Jebusites. And now the cry of the Israelites has reached me, and I have seen the way the Egyptians are oppressing them. So now, go. I am sending you to Pharaoh to bring my people the Israelites out of Egypt." (Exodus 3:7–10)

For Moses, God gave a crystal-clear call to be His instrument to free His people, but there was no mention of Pharaoh's resistance, "bricks without straw," the people blaming Moses, plagues, death, and the desert! The lack of full disclosure of the future didn't negate God's calling to Moses. They were features of the call that God didn't share at the beginning. It's the same for us: God seldom gives us more than a glimpse of the next bend in the road, and sometimes, not even that. We certainly don't expect detours! It is very common and very wrong to assume that if things aren't going smoothly in our ministries that we've somehow missed God's calling ...or at least His best for us.

SURPRISING BENEFITS OF ADMITTING OUR LIMITATIONS

Virtually every magazine ad and televi-sion commercial has two messages. Sure, they're selling toothpaste, beer, cars, and financial products, but the beautiful, happy people in them tell the audience that those products and services will give them a life without limits, full of power, popularity, and pleasure. I think those messages have seeped into the American psyche and con-

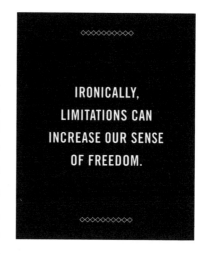

IRONICALLY, LIMITATIONS CAN INCREASE OUR SENSE OF FREEDOM.

vinced us that we shouldn't have any limitations, and if we're Christians, surely God doesn't want us to have any limitations! That's baloney, and dangerous baloney at that.

Admitting our limitations helps us grow. Coming to grips with our limita-tions brings us back to reality and enables us to trust God more fully and specifically with the challenges we face. A few years ago, I read a story about a famous photographer who set aside her huge bag of lenses and filters and used only her 35mm camera to take pictures. Some people were surprised by her sparse equipment, and she explained that taking a fixed-lens camera made her a better photographer. With it, she was forced to carefully analyze every aspect of placement, lighting, distance, and expo-sure. Her limitations caused her to notice more, be more precise, and develop her skills.

Ironically, limitations can increase our sense of freedom. The late Chris-tian financial counselor Larry Burkett told a story, now familiar to many, of kids in a kindergarten next to a busy highway. The children had a large playground, but it had no fences. The children stayed close to the building because they were afraid of the busy traffic just past the grass. In *Starting Out Right*, Burkett writes, "At last the principal of the kindergarten had a six-foot chain-link fence installed around the play yard. The next day when the children went out for recess, they played right up against the fence. The fence restricted their freedom, but it provided a safe boundary that allowed them the maximum limits of the playground."[1] The fence didn't inhibit their freedom; it expanded their sense of freedom. In the same way, knowing our limitations makes us wise so we don't take foolish risks (or at least as many of them), and then we'll have more freedom to do what God has called us to do. We want to reach the world for Christ, but our resources are a bit short of reaching that goal, so we focus on our community and one or a few places in the world where we can devote some resources to make a real difference. If we are driven to try to do too much, sooner or later we'll crash and burn. But if we recognize the "fences" of limited money, manpower, and time, we can wholeheartedly dive into the specific tasks God gives us.

A number of church planters have come into Mt. Pleasant, but several have failed because they tried to directly compete with Seacoast. They didn't have the resources to compete effectively. It would have been wise for those pastors to embrace their limitations and emphasize the uniqueness of their fellowships: they were small enough to build a strong sense of community in their whole congregations! Like *Cheers*, those churches would have been places "where everybody knows your name, and they're always glad you came." Those pastors didn't observe their fences and use their limitations to find creative solutions.

---

1   Larry Burkett, *Starting Out Right* (Colorado Springs: David C. Cook, 2015), p. 62.

Constraint stimulates creativity. Phil Hansen was an artist whose style was pointillism, using small dots of color to produce amazing paintings. His painting, though, caused nerve damage in his dominant hand. Without the ability to create art, Hansen became deeply discouraged. Later, a neurologist recommended that he "embrace the shake," advice that gave him new hope, changed his perspective, and reinvigorated his career. In his inspir-

ing TED talk, he explains that he now uses unconventional materials (even live worms and hamburger grease) and bizarre "canvases" (including stacks of Starbucks cups, bananas, and his own body). He videos himself creating the art, and his neurological problem, the shaking, has been integrated as part of the creative process. One of his most important contributions is his ability to inspire creativity in those who experience significant limitations.[2]

I talked with a man who is an executive in one of world's largest tech companies. One of the topics of conversation was Seacoast's hiring policies and process. He explained that his company doesn't look for people who require all the resources to do a job. Instead, they look for people who are committed to get the job done with whatever resources are at hand. Executives and managers in his company sometimes assign projects to teams and

2   For more on Phil Hansen, see his TED talk at: https://www.ted.com/talks/phil_hansen_embrace_the_shake . . . and read about him at: https://www.ted.com/speakers/phil_hansen

intentionally limit their resources so they have to find innovative ways to accomplish them. When people have almost unlimited resources—and let's face it, that's really what we all want!—they don't have to find novel solutions. Creativity, then, is just desperation in a pretty package.

THE BIRTH OF MULTI-SITE

Seacoast passed the 2000 mark in 1999, and by the next year, about 2300 attended our church. Our auditorium seated 500, so we had five services each weekend. As you can imagine, our staff was running ragged. So was I. If we were going to survive, we had to build so we could have fewer ser-vices. Our church was on a 14-acre tract. Next to us was a tract of 16 acres that I'd had my eye on for years. I had talked to the owner many times, and he always turned me down. Finally, he grimaced, "What part of 'No!' do you not understand?" (I'm slow, but I got the impression he didn't want to sell his land to us.)

We found another tract of 45 acres, and we prepared to build. In our research, we discovered that there could only be one entrance and one exit from the property, so it would take 45 minutes for a family to come and leave a service. Obviously, that doesn't work. I called a time-out, and we stopped all our planning. I told our church that we were having problems with our new property and our plans for a new church building, and I called us to a 17-day fast to seek the Lord's direction. (It was 17 days because Thanksgiving was coming up, and nobody wants to fast on that day!)

On the fifteenth day of our fast, the owner of the 16 acres next to our church called and asked, "Are you still interested in my land?"

I immediately responded, "Yes. Yes, we are!"

We bought his land, tabled all our plans for the other property, and sold it for a nice profit. I was really excited to build a new facility on our 30 acres. As we got new architectural plans, I began to notice articles about communities on the West coast that were changing zoning so churches couldn't build in prime places. I thought, *Yeah, but that's the West coast. It'll never happen here.*

As those who build large facilities know, it takes a long time to do all the site planning, fine-tune the architectural drawings, and get permits—and of course, raise money. We had been in this process for about a year when election day came. The newly elected city officials had run on a platform of keeping Mt. Pleasant small and quaint. In other words, they were going to scale back growth in the city. They chose our project as an example to developers and builders that they meant business.

Soon, I saw articles in the city newspaper that Seacoast was planning to build a monstrosity "twice the size of Walmart." That was during an era when Walmart was getting a lot of bad press for causing mom and pop stores to go out of business. Having Seacoast's name associated with Walmart wasn't a plus in public perception!

Yes, there were traffic jams every Sunday and Wednesday night on the two-lane road in front of our church, but the city had already begun expanding the road to five lanes, so this problem was going to vanish very soon. It didn't matter. Articles ignored the ongoing road construction and warned that the traffic jams would be far worse with our new and larger building. One of the city officials was quoted saying that Seacoast had outgrown Mt. Pleasant . . . which was a not-too-subtle way of saying we should leave!

When the city council voted on our building permits, they turned us down, and to boot, they changed the zoning so we could never build on the 30 acres we owned. One man on the council told someone, "I'm going to make Greg Surratt's life miserable. That's what I live for." (He didn't know the guy he told was a friend of mine.) He did his best. He introduced a proposal that required Seacoast to plant a dense buffer of trees at least 75 feet wide (so no one can see through it) starting at the highway right-of-way all across the front of our church. He didn't want people to even know we exist! The proposal passed, so we had to invest in planting a forest instead of building a new facility. It wasn't fair at all. The shopping center next to our church was required to have a 15-foot buffer of trees that were spaced out so people driving by could easily see the signs on the stores.

We were stuck. We couldn't build on the land we'd bought, and the city was adamant that they didn't want us to grow. In fact, they were punishing us for growing. When all this transpired, I was shocked and discouraged. I went to my office to think and pray. I felt the bone-deep heartache of disappointment. I pulled down the shade and turned on some country music. I wondered how I could tell our church people that our dreams had died when a majority of hands were raised at a city council meeting.

My gloom didn't lift very quickly, and I guess it was obvious to a lot of people. One day after church a lady came up to me and said, "Pastor, it's okay to sit on the pity potty as long as you don't sit long enough to get ring around the hiney!"

During this dark season, I learned one of the most valuable spiritual lessons of my life: Nothing surprises God. He has never had to say, "My bad. I didn't see that coming." It doesn't matter what the surprise is to us—money troubles, a wayward teenager, a health problem, staff conflict, or anything else—it didn't catch our all-knowing, all-loving Father by surprise. And if the problem didn't surprise Him, we can be sure He already had planned a solution before the problem ever surfaced. God hadn't abandoned us, and He wasn't ignoring us. He knows, He cares, and He provides...in His way and in His timing. This spiritual truth lifted my spirits and gave me hope again.

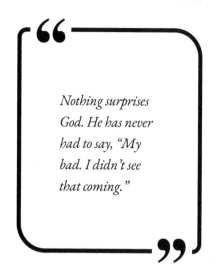

Nothing surprises God. He has never had to say, "My bad. I didn't see that coming."

Part of this insight is the realization that God is the only one who is omniscient. I'm not. This gives me a reason to pause before I put a "good" or "bad" label on a situation because, though it may look bad, God is always working for our good. He knows the future, I don't. That's what Romans 8:28 is about. And that's what happened to us: The roadblock in our building plans that I thought was a disaster led to perhaps our biggest blessing to the body of Christ. We couldn't build on our land, so the only way we could grow was by having multiple campuses.

We didn't invent multi-site churches, but we were on the leading edge—not because I'm such a fantastically creative visionary, but because we had no other choice. A few years earlier, I had attended a Leadership Network conference in Denver, and Larry Osborne led a breakout session on "video

venues." The concept hadn't really caught on yet, so there were only about five of us in the room. Larry described how his church was using video at other sites to create branches of community still under the authority and leadership of his church. I was interested, but I didn't see how we might use it. Later, I heard that Willow Creek was experimenting with "offsites." Same concept, different label, city and church. Someone told me about a church in Rockford, Illinois, that solved the problem of not having a pastor by showing videos of sermons preached at Willow Creek over the previous years.

When the city council blocked our way and I began to come out of my "miry pit," I remembered those stories and Larry's concepts. I asked my brother Geoff, who served on our pastoral team, to go with me to observe multi-site churches and see if the concept might be a solution for us. (At the time, Geoff thought the idea was ridiculous, but he agreed to go anyway.) I also invited Byron Davis, a retired CEO for Fisher-Price, to fly across the country with us to San Diego so we could meet with Larry Osborne. He showed us how it works to have church in several locations with the same culture and leadership. Byron, Geoff, and I then took a red-eye to Chicago and drove to Rockford. We changed clothes in the bathroom of the car dealership where the church met, and we joined the church congregation as they worshipped with their band and then watched a three-year-old sermon by John Ortberg. The question I always ask myself when I attend another church is, "Would I go to church here?" At Rockford, my answer was "Yes!" They had great music, small groups, a sense of community, and outstanding teaching—what's not to love about that?

We then drove back to Chicago to attend one of Willow Creek's offsite campuses. At that point, they hadn't figured out how to make it work.

They showed a video of the entire Willow Creek service, including music, announcements, and the message. The only people live on stage at the off-site were three people doing karaoke with the song leader on the screen. It wasn't great, but there were 300 people in the room who called it their church. If they felt good about that, there was hope we could create something that might work near Charleston, South Carolina.

When Byron and I got back home, I told our staff my plans: we were going to rent part of the shopping center next door to the church. (In hindsight, I realized that renting a building right next door isn't the best idea for your first off-site campus. I'd never recommend this idea to anyone!) My brother Geoff didn't need the benefit of hindsight. He instantly announced, "That's the worst idea I've ever heard. Why would anyone go to a rented building to watch you on video?"

"Great question," I told him. "You and Byron can figure it out. You're in charge of the new services."

On Sunday mornings in the shopping center, we had live music and a video of the previous Saturday night's sermon at what became known as Seacoast's broadcast campus. Soon, the services at this new facility were packed with people. (Eventually, Geoff wrote the book that's now considered the bible of multi-site.)

Years before this next-door launch, we had planted a church in Columbia, the state capitol. The pastor called me one day and said, "Greg, I'm burned out. I'm going to quit."

I told him, "You can't quit. I don't have anyone to replace you."

After a silent moment or two, he asked, "Well, what if we tried that video thing you're doing next to your church?"

I responded, "That'll never work. It works next door, but not two hours away."

He insisted, "Well, then I quit."

Faced with his determination, I gave in: "Okay, let's try it."

A few days later, we packed some of our staff in a van and headed to Columbia for a Wednesday night service to explain how multi-site would work. They had never heard of such a thing, and we couldn't point them to a lot of glowing examples. Almost everybody (except their pastor) concluded it was a really dumb idea. We called it "Bloody Wednesday." People in the church that night questioned my sanity and my motives. They assumed it was a power play to get my face in front of more people and make a name for myself outside the Charleston area. The look on their faces and the words they spoke were of contempt and disgust: "Who do you think you are?" "We've never even heard of Seacoast!" "Why are you trying to take over at our church?"

At the end of the meeting, I told them, "We'd love to help your church survive and thrive, but if you have to have a live speaker, there are a lot of churches in your city where you can go." They agreed to give it a shot, and they had 300 their first week. That number may not sound very impressive until you realize they had been averaging about 50. It eventually grew so large that it launched another campus in the Columbia area.

On the drive up to Columbia, Byron had told me, "Let me say something to you. If this concept doesn't work in Columbia, it doesn't mean it won't work in other places. But if it works in Columbia, it'll work anywhere. No matter what happens tonight, don't give up on this idea." Well, it worked in Columbia, and today it's working in cities and towns around the globe. I'd like to take credit for the idea, but I can't. The seed came from Larry Osborne, and the fuel to make it happen came from abject desperation. We had no other choice.

FACE THE FACTS

I encourage pastors and their staffs (or key volunteers) to analyze their church's strengths and limitations. Here's my advice: Be ruthlessly honest about the limitations that prevent you from moving from where you are now to where you believe God wants you to be. Don't sugarcoat the lack of resources, and don't over-spiritualize by insisting that God will provide in some magical way resources that solve every problem. He probably won't; instead, He'll almost certainly provide a creative solution.

"no MAtteR whAt hAppens tonight, Don't give up on this iDeA."

Your current limitations aren't a surprise to God. He wants to use them as a catalyst for your growth as a leader and your church's growth. In fact, your limitations are a surprise source of strength, but only if you look past the roadblocks to see new avenues open to you. As Paul assures us, God's power is made perfect in our weakness. Admit you're weak, and watch how God can release His wisdom, grace, power, and love in ways that amaze everyone involved.

Let me go back to the story about the trees we had to plant in front of our church. Every day when I walked across Long Point Road from our offices to the church, the stand of trees was a burr under my saddle. Whether the words formed in my mind or not, the emotion I felt was seething resentment: *This isn't fair! It's just not right!* A lot of wonderful things were happening at our church, but those trees...

One day as I made this trek, I sensed the Lord saying to me, "Every branch on those trees represents a multi-site church somewhere in America and in countless places around the world." That moment completely changed my walk through the trees each day. Resentment turned to gratitude that God, in His wonderful grace, would choose to let our church and me play a small part in multiplying churches around the world. Each branch now represents, in John's metaphor in Revelation, a lampstand of God's truth, grace, love, and power in a world that desperately needs Him. Our limitation has proved to be a blessing to countless people.

YOUR CURRENT
LIMITATIONS
AREN'T A
SURPRISE to
GOD.

THINK ABOUT IT

1

What are some magazine ads and television commercials that communicate that we shouldn't have any limitations? What's their underlying but very powerful promise?

....

....

....

....

....

....

....

2

How do Paul's insights in 2 Corinthians 12 apply to your current situation?

....

....

....

....

....

....

....

3

What are your current
limitations in money,
time, talent, and
other resources?

....

....

....

....

....

....

....

....

....

4

How frustrated have
you been about those
limitations? How
have your frustrations
affected you, your
family, your team, and
your church?

....

....

....

....

....

....

....

....

....

....

5

How have you seen
limitations stimulate
creative solutions in the
lives of other leaders?

....

....

....

....

....

....

....

....

....

....

....

....

....

....

....

....

....

....

....

....

6

Why is it crucial to
realize God isn't
surprised at any of
our roadblocks
and limitations?

....

....

....

....

....

....

....

....

....

....

....

....

....

....

....

....

....

....

....

7

What's your next step
to turn your limits
into strengths?

....

....

....

....

....

....

....

....

....

....

....

....

....

....

....

....

....

....

....

....

CHAPTER FOUR

UNCOVERING
HIDDEN DESIRES

Q: HOW CAN YOU GIVE PEOPLE WHAT THEY REALLY WANT
INSTEAD OF WHAT THEY THINK THEY WANT?

Years ago, I read an article by entrepreneur Mark Cuban titled, "Why You Should Never Listen to Your Customers." He explains that he worked with a company to create a product that was technically better than anything on the market. The customers loved it, and sales were very good. But the company then "made a fatal mistake. It asked its customers what features they wanted to see in the product, and they delivered on those features." Their competitors, though, had a vision of creating a better way of doing business, not just a better way of creating a product. They created products the customers didn't even know they wanted until they saw them, and their sales skyrocketed. Cuban concludes,

> Entrepreneurs need to be reminded that it's not the job of their customers to know what they don't...Instead, part of every entrepreneur's job is to invent the future....Your customers can tell you the things that are broken and how they want to be made happy. Listen to them. Make them happy. But don't rely on them to create the future road map for your product or service. That's your job. [1]

---

1   "Mark Cuban on Why You Should Never Listen to Your Customers," Mark Cuban, *Entrepreneur*, https://www.entrepreneur.com/article/222501

A BIGGER JOB IS TO GIVE THEM WHAT THEIR HEARTS LONG FOR, EVEN IF THEY CAN'T DESCRIBE IT YET.

If Henry Ford had polled people at the turn of the twentieth century to ask what they wanted in transportation, they would have said "faster horses." People can often describe a problem, but they usually expect an improvement on past solutions as the best answer. It often isn't. That's the genius of Steve Jobs. He created iMacs, iPods, iPads, and iPhones that were beyond what most people even thought they might want, but when they saw them, they had to have them. He didn't poll customers to see what they wanted; he invented the future of technology.

The same is true for pastors. If we poll our audience, they'll tell us what they think they want, and we can spend our lives trying to figure out how to fulfill the desires of every group in our congregations. But that's not wise. A bigger job is to give them what their hearts long for, even if they can't describe it yet.

WHAT DO THEY *REALLY* WANT?

This question sparked the most significant innovation in the history of Seacoast. In those very painful early days of our church, we experienced a gradual reverse exodus: week after week more people left the Promised Land. Some would call it a "Gideon's revival." This wasn't exactly my plan. What in the world was happening?

From the outset, we were a conglomerate of three different groups of people. Our sending church in Charleston was led by godly and gifted people and was a growing, biblically based, charismatic community of believers. About 55 people from that church came over to join our startup. A small, word of faith church in Mt. Pleasant was closing its doors the very day we planted Seacoast, and their pastor encouraged his 35 people to go to our church. (Years later when I told this story at a conference, a man came up to me after I spoke and said, "I'm the guy who was the pastor of that little church in Mt. Pleasant." I asked him if I'd portrayed him and the church accurately and graciously, and he said I did. I was glad . . . and relieved.) About 30 people who had previously attended an Episcopal church had a transforming experience with the Holy Spirit, and they received the left foot of fellowship from their priest. They had been meeting together without a leader, and they were eager to join us. The rest who came in those first weeks were unchurched people we had called to invite.

In the first six months of our church's life, as the numbers waned week after week, individuals or a few from each of these groups made appointments to talk to me. A man who had attended our sending church and represented several others from that group told me he didn't like the music in our services. I thought he meant it was too contemporary or too loud, but then he explained, "We always sang an anthem at our church in every service. I miss that. It meant so much to me." Of course, I knew what he was talking about since I'd been on staff there. It was "I Exalt Thee" by Jack Hayford. He was obviously disappointed when he told me, "We haven't sung it a single time in the three months I've been coming here. We don't have to sing it every week, but we need to sing it regularly." What he meant was, "We need to sing it regularly if my wife and I are going to stay." He was a successful businessman who gave generously, so this conversation had several layers of implications. In those days I wasn't the most diplomatic young pastor the world has ever known. I looked him in the eye and said boldly, "Our music is not for sale." The next week, his Mercedes and several others like it didn't drive into our parking lot on Sunday morning...or ever again.

Two ladies from the word of faith church came to see me. After we chatted for a few minutes, one of them delicately asked, "Pastor Greg, when are we going to do it." I knew exactly what she meant. She wanted to know when we were going to have the gifts of the Spirit manifest in our worship services, complete with people being slain in the Spirit. I explained that our church had a different emphasis to reach the unchurched, and we weren't going to do "church as usual." They weren't happy with my answer, so they left the church and took quite a few people with them.

Then three people from the band of renegade Episcopalians came to the office. Before they said a word, I knew what they were going to say. It doesn't take a prophet to figure that out. They were very kind, but they were direct. They wanted to know when we would make the Eucharist a major part of our regular worship services. I tried to accommodate them because their spirit was very positive and gracious. We scheduled an early service and asked an Episcopal priest to lead it. It didn't work very well at all, so we stopped. Soon, a number of those people were MIA.

It wasn't that *everybody* complained. The unchurched people had nothing to compare our church to, so they never griped — God bless them.

FIGURING IT OUT ⋯⋯⋯⋯⋯⋯⋯⋯⋯⋯⋯⋯⋯⋯⋯⋯⋯

All pastors have to wrestle with a wide range of expectations from different groups in their congregations. My situation wasn't unique, but it felt more precarious because we hadn't yet established our culture. Everyone thought they had a perfect right to give input and make it what they wanted it to be.

The three individuals and groups who came to see me said they wanted us to change to suit their tastes, but is that what they really wanted? In the middle of all those conversations, I thought long and hard about this issue. Is a change to the music or the way we structure the services going to revolutionize their lives and meet their deepest desires? No, what every person wants is to experience *the presence and power of Jesus.* Their requests were their best attempts to make that happen, even if they couldn't articulate the hidden but very real desires underneath their requests. They were asking for the package their encounter with Jesus came in the last time they experienced Him. The people from the sending church experienced the presence and power of Jesus when they sang "I Exalt Thee." Those from the word of faith church experienced it when they saw the gifts in operation. And the Episcopalians experienced the wonder of the presence and power of Christ in their liturgy. All of them had asked me to replicate the package, but they really wanted Jesus.

> EvERyoNE tHouGHt tHEy HAD A PERFECt RiGHt to GivE inPut AnD MAKE it wHAt tHEy wAntED it to BE.

The presence and power of Jesus is eternal—there's not a "use by" date on it. But the package it comes in is temporal—there's an expiration date. It changes from culture to culture and from generation to generation. The songs that seem so archaic to young people today were fresh and real to those of us who can remember the first time they were sung, and all the hymns were radically novel a century or two ago. Undoubtedly, a past generation turned up their noses at "Amazing Grace" because it wasn't familiar to them.

Innovation is inherently disruptive, but I've learned that disruption is absolutely necessary for the health of an organization. As I've observed churches over several decades, I've noticed that many of them plateau and decline after about 10 years of remarkable growth. Why? I think it happens because those leaders became comfortable with their processes and strategies, so they avoided anything disruptive. Before I understood this fact, disruption made me feel insecure, like what we were doing couldn't be right. At Seacoast, we've gone through three phases of innovation and disruption: planting a nondenominational church with contemporary music that's attractive and welcoming to unchurched people (which doesn't seem revolutionary at all now), launching multi-site campuses (ditto), and then, when Seacoast had grown to about 7,000, I sensed that we needed a fresh explosion of experimentation. I felt stale, and our services felt stale to me. Like most churches, we had four songs at the beginning, then the message, and a song to close. Surely, we could trust God to give us something fresh.

That year between Christmas and New Year's, I went to Starbucks to relax for a few minutes. The hectic pace before Christmas was over, and I needed some down time. As I sat drinking my coffee, a lady came up to me. She said, "I had a dream that you would be here today." Oh great, I thought, *this is going to be very interesting*. She asked, "Do you have time to talk?" I wanted to run and hide, but I must have nodded some kind of affirmation.

She sat down, and then lowered her voice: "Pastor, I need you to forgive me for something." I should have stopped her right there and said, "No problem. You're forgiven. Go in peace." But I didn't. She told me, "My husband and I are leaving Seacoast. We're being fed more at another church, and I wanted you to know why we're leaving." I don't think people understand how painful that statement is to a pastor. I was furious, but she wasn't finished. She then asked with saccharine sweetness, "Can I pray for you?"

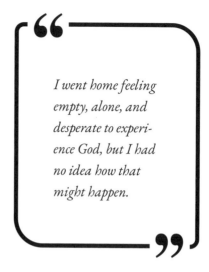

I went home feeling empty, alone, and desperate to experience God, but I had no idea how that might happen.

I thought about a sarcastic comment I could say to her, but self-control prevailed, and I said only, "I'm good. Thanks anyway."

I had gone to Starbucks to relax and enjoy a few minutes of quiet, but I left there deeply discouraged and angry. I thought about places I could go to hide from everybody and escape everything. Getting lost for a while would be easy. It was a tempting idea, but I soon realized I couldn't hide from myself.

I went home feeling empty, alone, and desperate to experience God, but I had no idea how that might happen. Soon after my encounter with the woman at Starbucks, I spoke at a John Maxwell leadership event in Scotland. (This was the first of several pivotal experiences within a six-month timeframe.) A friend at the conference asked me if I wanted to go on an adventure on a day off. I told him, "You bet. Count me in!" He took me to the Isle of Iona, where the gospel first came to Scotland. Monks in Ireland were church planters who traveled to many parts of Europe to tell people about Jesus, and they didn't have to travel very far to get to Scotland. They built a monastery on Iona, where the weather is terrible much of the year. On the day we went, it was raining hard and the wind was blowing a gale. The ferry captain told us, "I can get you there, but I can't promise to get you back." My friend and I looked at each other and shrugged as if to say, "Oh well, what's there to lose?"

When we got to the monastery, we saw a burial ground of ancient kings. I slipped into a little stone chapel to get out of the rain. As I stood dripping in the doorway, I noticed a lady standing in front of a cross that had small pieces of paper pinned to it. She was weeping. After a few minutes, she wrote something and pinned it to the cross. She left, and I went over to the altar. In that moment, I sensed the presence and power of Jesus. I didn't know why or how, and I didn't really care. All I knew was that I was in the awesome presence of God.

A few months later, John Maxwell asked me to speak at another event, this time in India. I looked at the possible stops between here and there, and I decided to stop in Paris because I'd never been to "The City of Lights." I scheduled enough time between flights so I could take a quick trip into the city. I went to the grand, Gothic cathedral of Notre Dame. Inside, I found people lighting candles as symbols of prayer. Some of them were crying, and all of them seemed to be captured by the moment. Suddenly, I was too. Though much of Europe has abandoned the Christian faith, God was meeting those people, and He met me in the same way. I was moved by the presence and power of Jesus. It was magnificent! Surely, the Spirit of the Lord was in that place.

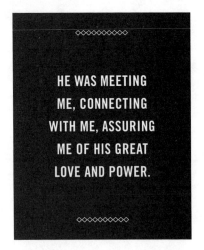

HE WAS MEETING
ME, CONNECTING
WITH ME, ASSURING
ME OF HIS GREAT
LOVE AND POWER.

Weeks later, I attended an Anglican church in our community, and as they do in every service, they celebrated the Eucharist, the Lord's Supper. Many Protestant traditions tack it on to a service or have it once a month on Wednesday or Sunday night, and quite often, there's little explanation to help people experience the wonder of Christ's sacrifice. We can argue about the different ways theologians have explained what happens, whether it's the "real presence" of Christ or symbolic or any of the other ways people understand it. None of that mattered to me. All I knew was that when I knelt at the altar and took the elements, a wonderful sense of God's presence came over me. He was meeting me, connecting with me, assuring me of His great love and power.

Soon after that day, I attended a friend's church. It's a charismatic church, and at the end of the service, he invited people to come forward to be anointed with oil for healing. He said that we often think only of physical healing, but God also wants to heal us spiritually and relationally. I was well aware of the hole in my heart, so with about a hundred others, I went to the front to be anointed. When my turn came, my friend asked, "What do you need from the Lord?"

I responded, "I don't even know how to say it. I just need you to pray for me." He put a drop of oil on his finger and touched my forehead, and he prayed. I've been in countless services like this before, but for some reason, this time God's presence was powerful. As I stood at the altar with this man's hand on my shoulder as he prayed, I had an almost palpable sense of the power and the warm presence of Jesus.

The next time I preached at Seacoast, I did what I always do: after my message, I went back to the sound booth during the final song. In that moment, I sensed God say to me, "Now is the time."

I asked, "The time for what?" I had no idea what He meant. Instantly, the Spirit brought a passage to mind. Through Isaiah, the Lord told His people:

> "These people come near to me with their mouth
> and honor me with their lips,
>   but their hearts are far from me.
> Their worship of me
> is based on merely human rules they have been taught.
> Therefore once more I will astound these people
> with wonder upon wonder;
> the wisdom of the wise will perish,
> the intelligence of the intelligent will vanish."
> (Isaiah 29:13–14)

I thought about the worship services at Seacoast, and it struck me that nothing in them "astounded these people with wonder upon wonder."

The next week, I announced, "In three weeks, everything at Seacoast is changing." I didn't tell them what it would be. Let me tell you, I never announce change before it's going to happen because about two-thirds of people are predisposed against change. But this time, I felt God wanted me to let them know something was coming.

HELPING PEOPLE CONNECT ·······

People may have thought I was going to resign, but whatever the reason, three weeks later the auditorium was packed. I shared the passage from Isaiah, and I told them, "We're changing the way we worship. We're going to invite God to astound us." I told them we were going to have two songs at the beginning instead of four. This would accomplish two objectives: it would give us more time for some new elements in the service, and it kept men from checking out mentally when the singing lasts too long for them. (I told our worship leaders to watch people beyond the first four rows. The people in the front sit there because they're all in, but behind them, a lot of people, especially men, tune out pretty quickly during the singing.)

After the campus pastor greets people, we have all the announcements on video so we can control the length of time spent on them. The message begins within the first ten or twelve minutes after the service starts. Some pastors have told me, "If we did that, I'd be preaching to empty seats." That's because many pastors have trained people that it's perfectly fine to come in 15 minutes late. At Seacoast, we actually start two minutes before the announced time for the service. Our people know that if they're not early, they're late.

> WhAt is GOD sAying to you? AnD How ARe you going to RespOnD to Him?

After the message, I now always explain that there are two questions each person needs to answer: What is God saying to you? And how are you going to respond to Him? To help them clarify their response, I may say something like this: "Some of you feel far from God today. Maybe you've never had a connection with Him. Some have had a connection with God in the past, but you've drifted a long way away. It's time to come home. I want you to whisper a prayer, 'God, I want you in my life.' You already know you're a sinner, and when you ask Him to come into your life, you're trusting in His grace to forgive you and His love to accept you. If that's your response, take a card in front of you and fill it out to let us know you've committed your life to Christ. We want to help you grow in your faith. Text the number on the screen, and we'll send you information that will be very valuable to your walk with Jesus."

At that point, I invite people to get up and go to one of the stations we've set up in the auditorium. At one of them, they can take a little piece of paper that represents them and pin it to a cross. If I've mentioned worry in my message, I may say, "When you pin that piece of paper to the cross, you're making a divine exchange: your worries for God's peace."

I then say, "Some of you have a friend you're concerned about. You wish that friend had been here this morning to experience the presence and power of Jesus. Go to the area where we have candles, and light one for your friend. The candle is a symbol of prayer. When you light it, say something like this: 'May the light of Jesus and the power of the Holy Spirit touch my friend.'" Seekers and Catholics are often eager to light a candle for someone they love.

I then tell our people, "Some of you need God to heal a broken heart, a disease, or an emotional trauma. James wrote, 'Is anyone among you sick? Let them call the elders of the church to pray over them and anoint them with oil in the name of the Lord. And the prayer offered in faith will make the sick person well; the Lord will raise them up. If they have sinned, they will be forgiven' (James 5:14–15). It's not that *you* need to have faith to heal; it's the *elders'* faith. Have you ever been so troubled that you didn't have any faith? Some people here will loan you theirs. Come and be anointed with oil. Our elders will pray for you."

Before they get up, I tell them, "And we're going to serve Communion today. You'll find a number of places around the auditorium where you can receive the elements and remember the sacrifice of Christ for you. That's where we celebrate the life, death, and resurrection of Jesus, because He's the source of everything good in our lives."

I have one more instruction: "Also around the room you'll find some offering boxes. Give generously because God has been so generous with you." Most of our people give online, but we want to give them an opportunity to give at church if they want to.

Finally, before they get up, I remind them, "And after a while, we're going to sing and celebrate an awesome God who loves you more than you can know. But first, answer those two questions: What is God saying to you? And how are you going to respond to Him?" At that point, people get up and go to many different parts of the room to respond to what God has put on their hearts.

This is an altar call for everybody. It's as powerful today as it was the first week we set up these places and invited people to respond. The variety of stations allows people to respond to their changing circumstances, and it never gets old.

Not long after we started this practice in our worship service, nine firefighters died in a blaze in Charleston. Except for the Twin Towers on 9-11, it was the greatest loss of life for firemen in American history. It happened on a Friday. That Sunday morning, I saw firemen in uniform throughout our congregation. When I gave the invitation, some of them went to the cross, many lit candles, some asked to be anointed with oil, and most of them remembered Christ's sacrifice by taking Communion. As I stood at the front and watched, I thought, *Thank God we've created an environment where these people can respond and in their own ways experience the presence and power of Jesus!*

Our oldest daughter Jenny always wanted to be a mother just like her Mom, but two tubal pregnancies seemed to close the door and shatter her dreams. She and her husband Ben talked with Debbie and me about the possibility of in-vitro fertilization. We believe that every fertilized egg is a person, so we had to process all this very carefully. Finally, she had one or two fertilized eggs implanted. We were so excited, and then we were crushed when we found out they didn't take. This happened time after time. Jenny told Debbie and me that she wanted to try again, and this time, she had two implanted. We didn't make any announcements, but on the following Sunday, Debbie and I lit two candles for Jenny and the babies during every service. The next morning, Jenny called to tell us the doctor said she was going to be a mom! This experience gave me firsthand knowledge of the kind of hurt people carry.

Giving them (and us) an opportunity to process the pain with God is incredibly valuable.

This way of inviting people to respond to God has totally disrupted the pattern of worship at Seacoast...in a remarkably good way. No matter how well or poorly the message goes, people have the chance to respond to God's voice and connect with Him in ways that transform their lives.

I didn't know why God chose to touch me when I stood before the cross in the stone chapel on that stormy day on Iona. I didn't know why God moved in my heart when I lit a candle at Notre Dame. I didn't know why I experienced the presence of Jesus at an Anglican Communion. I didn't know why I went forward to ask to be anointed and prayed for when I couldn't even articulate what needed to be healed. But it didn't matter why. All that mattered was that I longed to experience the presence and power of Jesus, and God showed up in those places.

As pastors, we know we aren't the only game in town. We try hard to have great music, but it's seldom terrific. We try hard to preach with power, but we know we aren't the most gifted communicators in the world. We try to administrate our churches in a way that brings out the best in people, but a lot of things fall through the cracks. None of that matters if we're giving people what they really want: opportunities to sense, to feel, to know, to be moved by the presence and power of Jesus.

Some people might ask, "Don't you feel at least a little presumptuous to impose your experiences on your church's worship style?" My answer is, "Yeah, maybe. But isn't that what leaders do? I'm sharing what God has done in me with the people I lead." I didn't read a manual or hear a talk at a conference that explained how to create times and spaces for all this to happen at Seacoast. It began with a raw sense of my own emptiness, and God orchestrated experiences that showed me He hadn't forgotten me. All I've done is translate what He did for me so that others can have the same opportunity.

> *All that mattered was that I longed to experience the presence and power of Jesus, and God showed up in those places.*

You don't need to do exactly what I've done, but please be open to the Spirit's desire to touch you and fulfill your genuine desire to know His presence. And then, listen to Him as He leads you to disrupt your worship services as you invite people to have these experiences week after week. (To see a video of this part of our service, go to Seacoast.org/response.)

MAKE ROOM

A historian of the Old Testament tells us about a remarkable scene in the life of the prophet Elisha. God's people were suffering from famine. Elisha often traveled through Shunem, and an older woman always invited him to eat with her and her elderly husband. She told her husband, "I know that this man who often comes our way is a holy man of God. Let's make a small room on the roof and put in it a bed and a table, a chair and a lamp for him. Then he can stay there whenever he comes to us" (2 Kings 4:9–10). That's what God wants from us—to make room for Him. When we do, God will fill the room. He may even give us blessings we would never have dreamed of.

In the life of the Shunammite woman, Elisha prayed and God miraculously gave her a son. She was thrilled, but later her son became gravely ill. She sent for Elisha, and he came to heal her son. The historian puts us in the scene:

> When Elisha reached the house, there was the boy lying dead on his couch. He went in, shut the door on the two of them and prayed to the LORD. Then he got on the bed and lay on the boy, mouth to mouth, eyes to eyes, hands to hands. As he stretched himself out on him, the boy's body grew warm. Elisha turned away and walked back and forth in the room and then got on the bed and stretched out on him once more. The boy sneezed seven times and opened his eyes.
>
> Elisha summoned Gehazi and said, "Call the Shunammite." And he did. When she came, he said, "Take your son." She came in, fell at his feet and bowed to the ground. Then she took her son and went out. (2 Kings 4:32–37)

The point is that we never get beyond our need for God's presence and power. Even when God has been very real to us, there will be struggles and heartaches. Sometimes, our worship is unabashed praise and gratitude, but quite often, our thanksgiving contains a measure of concern for ourselves or those we love.

Our services in Seacoast make room for God to work however people want to respond to Him, and we offer opportunities for people to express a wide range of hopes. In every service and in each person's life, I'm not sure what God is going to do, but I want to make plenty of room for Him.

1

What difference does it make for a pastor to grasp Mark Cuban's insight? "Your [people] can tell you the things that are broken and how they want to be made happy. Listen to them. Make them happy. But don't rely on them to create the future road map for your product or service. That's your job."

....

....

....

....

....

2

What are some of the "packages" Christians expect their pastors to create for them?

....

....

....

....

....

....

....

THINK ABOUT IT

3

To what extent do
your worship services
"astound" people with
the wonder of the
presence and power of
God? How can you tell?

....

....

....

....

....

....

....

....

....

4

What are some
times when you've
experienced God in
remarkable ways? How
did those moments
affect you?

....

....

....

....

....

....

....

....

....

5

Why do you think
people have responded
so positively to the
variety of opportunities
to express their hearts
to God at the end of our
services? What moves
them? What would
move you if you
were there?

....
....
....
....
....
....
....
....
....

6

How might you translate
at least some of these
ideas into opportunities
for people in your
church to sense the
presence and power
of Jesus?

....
....
....
....
....
....
....
....
....

CHAPTER FIVE

FINGERPRINTS

Q: WHAT LEGACY WILL YOU LEAVE BEHIND?

I enjoy reading lists. Over my years as a pastor, I've read lists of the fastest growing and biggest churches of each decade. I remember years ago when Elmer Towns wrote about the biggest Sunday school classes in the country. (It seems like that was eons ago.) One of the things I've noticed is that churches appear on these lists and sooner or later they vanish from them. Very seldom does a church remain vibrant more than two decades. They may still exist, but they become shadows of what they used to be.

One concept helps us understand how growth happens, and another explains how to prevent the decline. Most of us are familiar with a fly-wheel. It takes a lot of energy to get it moving, but as the rotations speed up, less energy is necessary to keep it going and even make it go faster. This is a perfect picture of the early years of these churches. The pastor, staff, and volunteers work like maniacs in the first years to get the church off the ground, and after a while, they hit their stride, form their culture, and the same amount of energy propels the church rapidly forward. But churches, like all living organizations, are creatures of entropy—the tendency toward randomness. Unless leaders are really sharp, success lulls

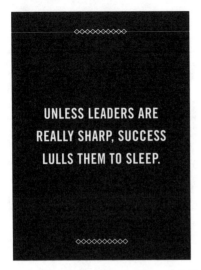

UNLESS LEADERS ARE REALLY SHARP, SUCCESS LULLS THEM TO SLEEP.

them to sleep. They rest on their reputation, stop innovating, and begin a long decline.

The second concept, one that gives insight about how to avoid organizational decline, is the Sigmoid Curve, conceived by Charles Handy and described in *The Age of Paradox*. In a *Forbes* article, "The Key to Growth: Transformational Change," Rebecca O. Bagley summarizes the idea: "The curve initially declines in a time of experimenting and learning, then rises in a period of growth and prosperity, and finally declines leading to the end. The key to sustaining a healthy life, a healthy business or a healthy region is to make a transformation to a new curve before the current one is too far in decline."[1] The key point for leaders is to anticipate the need for a fresh shot of energy and enthusiasm *during* a season of growth and *before* the decline begins. This seems counterintuitive to many leaders because they want to bask in the glow of their success, but if they don't begin a new cycle of growth, their organizations will plateau and begin to decline—and as we all know, it's much harder to change the trajectory when people feel disappointed than when they feel excited.

Three diagrams show the importance of understanding this concept. The first one depicts an organization's natural life cycle of beginning, an initial decline after the surge at the start, then a season of growth, decline, and finally, the death of the organization — or at least a long period of life support!

---

1   "The Key to Growth: Transformational Change,' Rebecca O. Bagley, *Forbes*, January 2, 2013, https://www.forbes.com/sites/rebeccabagley/2013/01/02/the-key-to-growth-transformational-change/#6fa7f4836b8c

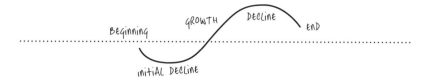

The second curve shows the point in the middle of the period of growth when a wise leader anticipates the need to inject fresh ideas and plans into the organization. The gray area is the time of tension when the leader is still promoting the current cycle of growth while at the same time starting a new cycle.

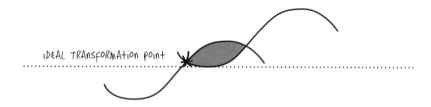

The third curve shows where most leaders finally realize they need to do something to add energy to the organization. By then, enthusiasm has ebbed, resources are probably spent, and they're trying to turn a ship that's headed in the wrong direction.

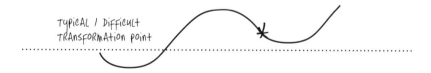

How many times do leaders need to anticipate decline and infuse the organization with fresh ideas and spark enthusiasm for a bigger goal? As often as they have seasons of growth. If they keep anticipating these pivotal moments during growth and invest their energy and creativity into new plans, the upward curves can keep going until the Lord returns!

OUR DREAM

My vision, and the vision of all of us at Seacoast, is to be a prevailing church for many generations. This is one of the reasons the Association of Related Churches (ARC) was created. A group of us wanted to pool our resources to inspire and equip new generations of church leaders. We want to be givers, not takers. We're committed to give a portion of all the money that comes into our churches to fund life-giving churches in every community, and we want to share all we've learned so young pastors become great pastors. That's a goal that both inspires and challenges me every day.

In addition to the formation of ARC, I also wanted to create a strategy to transition Seacoast to competent, godly leaders for the next generation. I've seen pastors hang on to their positions too long. There are many possible reasons, including lack of financial resources after leaving the church, they don't want to admit it's time for someone else to lead, no one is bold and loving enough to speak the truth that it's time to go, they're comfortable in their role, or they're afraid their lives will be empty if they don't keep their role as the senior pastor. Of all the many reasons, I believe the top two are money and identity—pastors want to keep their roles because they need the income, and they want to stay because being a pastor gives them a sense of meaning and purpose. Too often, churches and denominations fail to meet both of these needs: they don't give older pastors adequate financial resources, and they don't provide attractive off-ramps of meaningful ministry after they leave the pastorate. The solutions to these problems aren't easy or simple, but finding good answers is essential so pastors can look to the future instead of the past. At Seacoast, we offer a 401k to all our staff, and I almost beg people to take advantage of it. I tell them, "It's free money!" This is part of our effort to solve the first common problem, and through ARC, we're always looking for opportunities to involve retired pastors so they can invest their wisdom and experience in the lives of younger men and women.

A pastor who refuses to leave is one of the biggest causes of organizational decline. It seems that everyone but the pastor knows it's time to go. I didn't want to make this mistake and create this problem. I also saw many pastors who created a big hole when they left because they didn't select, equip, and train leaders to replace them. Some of those senior pastors were wonderful on stage, and that's what attracted a crowd, but they simply had no inclination or skill to train leaders.

The life of Caleb is a wonderful example of the impact of an older leader. He was one of the 12 spies who came back with a report of the Promised Land. He and Joshua were the only ones who believed God that they could conquer the land, so the people wandered in the desert for 40 long years until everyone in that generation was dead—everyone except Joshua and Caleb. As God's people crossed the Jordan and began fighting to take the land, Caleb didn't want to sit on the sidelines. He told Joshua, "So here I am today, eighty-five years old! I am still as strong today as the day Moses sent me out; I'm just as vigorous to go out to battle now as I was then. Now give me this hill country that the LORD promised me that day. You yourself heard then that the Anakites were there and their cities were large and fortified, but, the LORD helping me, I will drive them out just

> *When I looked at our leadership and our congregation, I could tell the church was graying with me. That's not a good dominant color for a church!*

as he said" (Joshua 14:10–12). When Caleb was a younger, stronger man, he could have climbed that mountain and whipped every man on it. But when he was 85, he had more wisdom than strength. He gave the warriors an incentive to help him: "I will give my daughter Aksah in marriage to the man who attacks and captures Kiriath Sepher" (Joshua 15:16). He still got the job done, but in a different way than he would have before.

Only a few years ago when I looked in the mirror, I saw a guy who had been full of vitality for a long time but whose energy had, shall we say, subsided a bit. When I looked at our leadership and our congregation, I could tell the church was graying with me. That's not a good dominant color for a church! Like Caleb, I can still take mountains, but maybe not ones that are as tall as before, and certainly not in the same way as before. Through an enlightening but painful process, I got a clearer picture of how God might use me for the rest of my life. I met with a godly life coach for two days. He asked me to analyze how God usually spoke to me and how He tended to use me. In these conversations, he explained the seasons of a man's life articulated by author and speaker John Eldredge[2]:

- The *adolescent* (teen years) is an explorer who learns how to develop genuine friendships.

---

2   Described in "Moral Manhood—Eldredge Six Stages & Ethical Learning," Duane Covrig, May 17, 2013, http://www.adventistethics.com/moral-manhood-eldredge-six-stages/

- The *warrior* (20s and 30s) identifies enemies and the battles worthy of his zeal and skill.

- The *lover* (20s and 30s) finds affection and makes a commitment for a lifetime.

- The *king* (40s and 50s) shapes a vision and leads people to accomplish big goals.

- The *sage* (60s +) uses all of his experiences and wisdom to help others become warriors, kings, and sages.

In those two days, I realized I was in the middle of a transition from king to sage, and it was really hard to face. I wondered if there was anything for me on the other side of being "the guy" at Seacoast. When I came home from those two days of self-examination, I was still in a fog about the future, but God didn't leave me there very long. Over the next few weeks, a number of people approached me with prophetic words. They said different things, but the common thread was this: "Pastor Greg, I don't know if this resonates with you or not, but I think the Lord wants to tell you that your next season will be your greatest season." Yeah, that resonated with me pretty well. Gradually, I believed God that my next season was as a sage, and it wasn't going to be just okay; it was going to be really good! I needed to look for opportunities to live out that specific role instead of accepting every invitation to speak at events. Being a sage would involve some speaking, but even more, it would put me in small groups of pastors for days at a time where we could peel off the layers of self-protection and get to the heart of what God wants to do in each leader's life.

16 CHURCH PLANTERS ON A FISHING RETREAT IN MONTANA   2015

As I write this, I recently came back from a fishing trip to Montana with a group of pastors. Actually, fishing was a small part of the equation. We spent hours and hours talking, sharing stories, and asking and answering questions. I loved pouring into their lives! (I stayed up until 3:00 in the morning playing cards and talking with three guys. It was wonderful.) When I got home, I was exhausted but thrilled. I walked in the door and told Debbie, "I'm built for this! I love it!"

> When I got home, I was exhausted but thrilled. I walked in the door and told Debbie, "I'm built for this! I love it!"

Being a pastor can be an incredibly lonely role. Young leaders need good friends around them and they need a sage to serve as a father speaking into their lives. The friends provide release valves for the pressure they feel, and the sage provides affirmation, encouragement, and direction when they wonder which way to go. Brothers in Christ may sometimes compete, but spiritual fathers complete their sons in the faith. (Actually, it's very unhealthy when spiritual fathers compete with their spiritual sons.) Many young pastors have "unconscious competence"—they're really good at what they do, but they don't know why. A sage can help them turn this into "conscious competence" so they can train others in their talents.

In the last few years, Seacoast has been getting younger instead of older. I've changed roles, and we've trained and placed some wonderful young leaders who are doing a fantastic job. Today, you won't find my fingerprints directly on the people, but they're all over the young men and women who lead them. I may or may not be able to build the church of the future, but I can definitely build the young leaders who will lead them.

BRASS TACKS ·········

When I speak on this topic, pastors invariably come up to ask me to give them more specific applications. No matter what stage of a church's life, our most important role is finding, hiring, training, placing, and shepherding leaders. Those we lead determine the trajectory of the church, and they become our legacy.

*** FiRSt hiREs ***

When we launched Seacoast three decades ago, my partners in this endeavor were my wife Debbie and my best friend Terry Hilgers. Terry and I have very similar talents in creativity and conceptual analysis. Both of us had all kinds of crazy ideas, and we worked together very well. The people leading our music were terrifically talented and had jobs in the marketplace, and they served our church for free for the first eight years. Surprisingly, one of the things that propelled our growth was when Terry felt led to leave and become a senior pastor. He moved to Aiken, South Carolina, and I felt like part of me left with him. I dreaded doing ministry without my sidekick. To replace him, we hired two people who had very different talents than Terry and me—one had gifts in pastoral care, and the other was a powerful evangelist. Soon, I realized how much Seacoast needed people with gifts that are very different from mine.

My view of the priority of hiring at a church plant is probably different from most people. I believe the pastor's first priority should be an administrative assistant, paid or volunteer. Years ago, I had a conversation with my administrative assistant. I asked, "Who do you think is the most important staff member at Seacoast?"

She looked a little surprised, and she said, "Well, it's obviously you."

"Exactly!" I was glad she got that right. "And who is the second priority?"

"The worship leader."

"Most people would assume that's the case," I responded, "but I don't think so." I let that sink in for a second, and then I explained, "Here's my point: if my role is so important, wouldn't it make sense that a church invest its first resources in a person who could make the person with my role even more effective?"

Let me go farther out on this limb. I believe that it's probably best for the administrative assistant to be virtual, especially for a startup. If you think for a minute, the reasons are clear: First, a virtual assistant is usually more efficient because there aren't all the distractions of working in the same office with the pastor. Second, you pay that person only for time spent working, not for "down time" that can absorb a lot of a person's day. And third, a competent assistant can take a tremendous load off the start-up pastor who often tries to do far too much himself. A virtual assistant can do almost everything someone in the office can do, and do it more efficiently and for less cost.

An assistant who lives a thousand miles away can make appointments just as easily as one who is sitting in the next office. I never set my own appointment schedule for one simple reason: I've screwed it up far too many times in the past. As I'm writing this, I admit that just yesterday I was an hour late to an appointment simply because I wrote down the wrong time. Sadly, that's not an isolated instance. (Did I mention I'm graying?)

Quite often, people come up to me after church or at a restaurant and say, "Pastor, I'd like to meet with you. What time would be convenient?" If I give them a time right then, there's a very good chance I'll double book, get the time wrong, or forget where I put the piece of paper I jotted it down on. Even when my close friends want to meet with me, I say, "I'd love to. Would you mind running that through Kathy? She knows my schedule, and she can make it work." Some people who said they wanted to meet with me never follow up with a call to Kathy. Maybe they were just being polite, or maybe the need passed.

A virtual assistant can screen a pastor's emails, and once a week (or whenever it's necessary), they can have a video conference to go over details. There's one more benefit of having a long-distance assistant: you don't become emotionally connected with that person. No, we never intend for it to happen, but it does. It's easy to spend far more time with an assistant than with a spouse. Eliminate even the possibility of temptation, drift, and sin. If the assistant is in another state or country, that problem doesn't exist.

As the church grows, my subsequent hires would be in this order: a worship leader, kids' pastor, a next generations' pastor for middle and high school students, small groups pastor, and finally, a person to handle the finances.

*** Picking the Right People ***

Far too often, pastors rely on personal preference in hiring staff members. Certainly, the chemistry is important, but many pastors have abysmal records in hiring great staff members. A number of fine organizations have tools and processes to help leaders find and hire the right people.

I'll defer to them for many of the specifics, but let me at least give a few principles.

First, be wary of hiring people who are just like you. No, don't hire people who disagree with everything you say and do, but look for balance. I loved working with Terry Hilgers, but in retrospect, we were probably too much alike. When we hired the other two people who had gifts that are different from mine, our growth accelerated.

Second, use a process. Don't just meet with someone a friend recommended and after a pleasant hour offer the job. Get others involved, especially people who are known to be intuitive and shrewd, and who see things from a different angle than you do . . . like your spouse! Even if your church is small—check that: especially if your church is small—go through a rigorous screening process to make sure you find the person who fits the role your church needs him or her to play.

Third, be sure to have a number of candidates to consider. Don't close the offer until you have "enough" people who are willing to go through the résumé and interview process. How many is enough? That depends on a number of factors, but err on the side of having more instead of fewer. Have a wide range of people interview promising candidates, including pastoral staff, administrative assistants, board members, and of course, people on the team the person will lead. If possible, find three candidates who you think will be

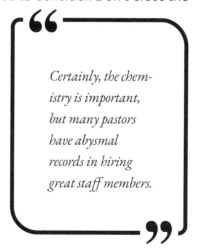

Certainly, the chemistry is important, but many pastors have abysmal records in hiring great staff members.

really good in the role, and then have a second round of interviews so you can get the best feedback to make the decision.

Fourth, don't hire too many too soon. When churches hire too many staff members, they take the place of volunteers who could be doing the job almost as well, and in some cases, even better. The growth of the church is directly proportional to the number of volunteers serving throughout the church. A leadership principle at Seacoast is: "We can't afford to pay people to do the work of the ministry." We need to pay staff members to "prepare God's people for works of service, so that the body of Christ may be built up until we all reach unity in the faith and in the knowledge of the Son of God and become mature, attaining to the whole measure of the fullness of Christ" (Ephesians 4:12–13). I believe it's true: "What's a burden to you could be a blessing to someone else." Having too many staff members robs people of the privilege and joy of serving God. Find the tension point where you have so many volunteers that you really need another staff member to give them resources and direction.

Fifth, watch for "volunteer creep"—that is, hiring people to do what they were doing effectively and gladly as volunteers. Yes, we value their contributions, and yes, we appreciate their selfless service, but the church grows primarily because people like them are thrilled to serve. We don't have to hire them to show our appreciation. Our church is a "volunteer led" organization. That's how we've grown, and that's how we'll continue to grow. Money—for more programs and more staff—promises to be the solution to every problem, but it's not. Volunteers are the most important resource of a church. In fact, a good question for pastors to ask is, "What are we paying people to do that volunteers can do just as well or even better?" (If your staff members are reading this, I think I just heard a few of them gulp!)

MONTANA FISHING SMALL GROUP EATING TOGETHER   2017

*** SENDING ***

I have an open-door philosophy about staff members planting churches and taking roles in other churches, but I require one thing: I want to be the first person to know, not the last. If I'm first, I'll break out the pompoms and lead the parade. If I'm somewhere down the list, let me just say I'm not as enthusiastic. If I'm not the first, I know there's very little trust, and that really hurts. Thankfully, that hasn't happened very often.

At one level, I understand the hesitancy of some staff members to tell the senior pastor they're considering a role at another church. They've heard stories, just as I have, of staff members who were treated with disrespect, and even contempt, for being "disloyal" because they wanted to go somewhere else. That's not going to happen at Seacoast — we don't punish people for following God's call. The harvest field is just a little bigger than Mt. Pleasant, South Carolina, and I'm thrilled to send people wherever God leads them...as long as they trust me with the truth and treat me with respect.

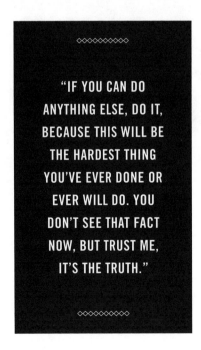

"IF YOU CAN DO ANYTHING ELSE, DO IT, BECAUSE THIS WILL BE THE HARDEST THING YOU'VE EVER DONE OR EVER WILL DO. YOU DON'T SEE THAT FACT NOW, BUT TRUST ME, IT'S THE TRUTH."

When young pastors tell me they want to plant a church, I'm very honest with them. I tell each one, "If you can do anything else, do it, because this will be the hardest thing you've ever done or ever will do. You don't see that fact now, but trust me, it's the truth."

People often ask me what's the difference between the qualifications for a campus pastor and a church planter. A campus pastor in our system has to be a good communicator, but a church planter must be a gifted communicator. How can you tell? By the responses of people. Those who are good communicators get positive feedback from family and friends, but gifted speakers move people they don't know and who have never heard them before. One staff member came to me and said, "I want to be a senior pastor."

I asked, "Tell me about your communication skills."

"I think I have the gift of public speaking."

I asked, "Does anybody have the gift of listening to you?"

He looked a bit surprised, so I followed up, "Tell me. What do people say about your speaking ability?"

"They say I'm getting better."

His response made everything clear to me. I told him lovingly but bluntly, "Brother, that's not good enough. You'll be in a world of trouble if you don't have communication gifts. I'm telling you this for your own good and for the good of the church." He wasn't ready, but that doesn't mean he isn't valuable to the kingdom or a particular church. It only means God hasn't given him the talents he needs to serve as a church planter or senior pastor. He didn't take my advice. He became the pastor of a church, but in a couple of years, it was obvious to everyone that he didn't have the skills he needed.

*** Letting People Go ***

I'm not very good at firing people. I'm pretty sure the whisper around Seacoast is, "You have to murder at least two people for Greg to fire you." I've learned, though, to be slower to hire and quicker to fire. But my pastoral gifts prompt me to treat people I fire the way I'd want to be treated, with a strong blend of truth and grace.

Long before a painful conversation about termination, I make sure the staff member and I both understand what a good job looks like. Even if the person is performing adequately, he or she may not be living up to our cultural values (addressed in Chapter 2: love God, treat people right, get better, and maintain a great attitude). These values shouldn't come as a surprise because we reinforce them every month in our all-staff meeting. If I need to tell people they don't fit our culture, I can be specific and explain the disconnect between them and us.

We always try to make things work in some way for staff members at our church. We give them several months to bring their performance up to an acceptable standard. If the problem is with the culture, we try to determine if more time will help. In many cases, it won't, so we begin the termination process. But for most people who are struggling with their roles, they're just in the wrong place for their talents. We move them to a job where they can serve more effectively, and often that's a very good solution. For people who are trying hard and have a good attitude, if the role simply didn't work and we can't find another place, we're very generous with them as they leave us. We do our best to help them find a better role somewhere else. We assure them that this isn't a surprise to God, and He'll use the transition for good if they'll trust Him.

Leaving a strong, positive, enduring legacy doesn't just happen, and it takes more than hard work and sweat. We need a God-directed plan to build into the people He has entrusted to us, to create environments where they can thrive and where young people are both directed and freed to do all God has put in their hearts. If you're a young warrior, take the land God has put on your heart. If you're a king, lead with power and integrity. If you're a sage, share the wisdom God has given you over many years of walking with Him. Whoever you are and whatever stage you're in, think and pray about what kind of legacy you'll leave...because, of course, we all leave one.

GREG & HIS FATHER
HUBERT SURRATT
2018

SURRATT FAMILY
1988

LEAVING A STRONG, POSITIVE, ENDURING LEGACY DOESN'T JUST HAPPEN.

GREG & DEBBIE SURRATT 2018

IT TAKES MORE THAN HARD WORK & SWEAT.

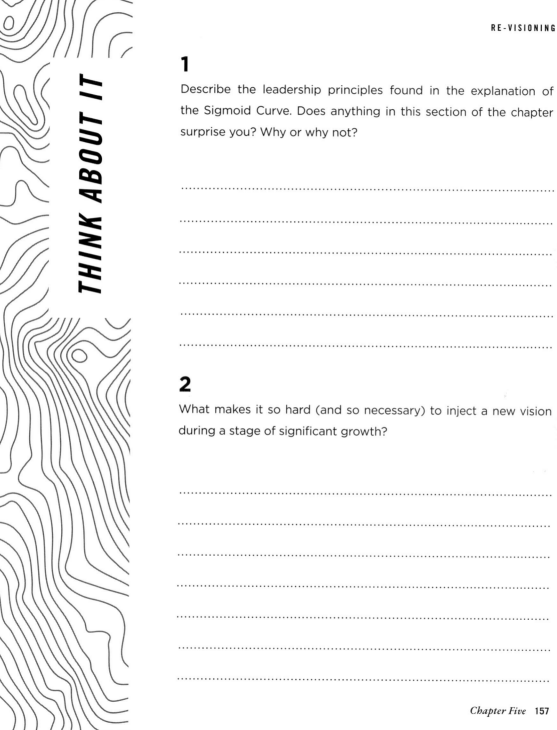

THINK ABOUT IT

1

Describe the leadership principles found in the explanation of the Sigmoid Curve. Does anything in this section of the chapter surprise you? Why or why not?

....

....

....

....

....

....

2

What makes it so hard (and so necessary) to inject a new vision during a stage of significant growth?

....

....

....

....

....

....

....

3

Where are you in the
seasons of leadership?
How well are you taking
advantage of your gifts
and experiences?

....
....
....
....
....
....
....
....
....

4

What changes (if any)
do you need to make in
your process of hiring
staff members?

....
....
....
....
....
....
....
....
....
....

5

Do you celebrate or
take it personally when
someone wants to leave
your team to take a role
somewhere else? Explain
your answer.

....
....
....
....
....
....
....
....

6

An organizational
consultant commented,
"I've never seen an
organization that didn't
need to fire at least one
person." What do you
think of that statement?
Is there anyone in your
church that you need to
fire? If so, how will you
do it?

....
....
....
....
....
....
....
....
....

CHAPTER SIX

BEYOND OUR WALLS

Q: HOW CAN the CHURCH BE ALL it CAN BE to the COMMUNITY?

God often uses turning points and difficulties to refine leaders so they can lead with power, wisdom, courage, and love. After Moses gave the reins of leadership to Joshua, God gave Joshua instructions to gather all the tribes for an assault to take the Promised Land. Crossing the Jordan was like drawing a line in the sand—this was it: they weren't turning back. Joshua told the people to ritually cleanse themselves because crossing the river was going to be an act of worship and obedience. He instructed the priests to pick up the Ark by its poles and lead the way. Crossing the Jordan was the climax of 40 years of rescue from Egypt, many miracles, and wandering in the desert. It would be one of the pivotal moments in the history of God's people. The Lord then told Joshua, "Beginning today I will show the people that you are their leader, and they will know that I am helping you as I helped Moses" (Joshua 3:7).

Past desolation in the desert and future battles in Canaan were the canvas on which God was going to paint the full picture of Joshua as a great leader, but on this day, God put His "seal of approval" on Joshua. Conquering the land wasn't going to be easy, and the people needed to have confidence in their leader. God was using this moment to build their confidence in Joshua and confirm that he was God's man. They were preparing to go far out of their comfort zones!

God has called us to go beyond our comfort zones, too, and He's looking for leaders to take His people to new places to do radical things. Almost always, it's beyond the walls of the church building.

FIRST (GRUDGING) STEPS

In 2001, just after the agonizing time when the city of Mt. Pleasant changed the zoning so we couldn't build a bigger facility and required us to plant a huge buffer zone of trees, the city planned to construct a skate park down the road from us. At the time, I was still seething, but Billy Hornsby, one of our staff members, told me, "You know, we don't have the best reputation in this town." That was an understatement, but he wasn't finished. "They see us as takers, not givers, and they think we cause more problems than we solve. We see ourselves as generous and noble, but people outside the church, rightly or wrongly, see us as sucking resources from the community. We don't pay taxes, we cause traffic jams, and we wanted to build a church twice the size of Walmart . . . at least, that's their perception." He let me think about that for a minute, and then he said, "That's our image. Let's change it."

I wanted to push back and say, "Billy, you don't get it. We're doing so much good for Mt. Pleasant. People are being saved, broken families are being restored, we have wonderful worship, we're growing, people's lives are being changed, and we're putting tons of resources into the people of this city," but I didn't say any of that because I knew he was right. At the time, we had about 2300 people in the church. There were 600,000 in the Greater Charleston area, so of course, very few of them had experienced the great things happening at Seacoast. All they knew was what they read in the local newspaper and how they suffered when they got stuck in a traffic jam on the road outside our church. They were skeptical... and annoyed with us. And these were the people we were trying to reach for Jesus!

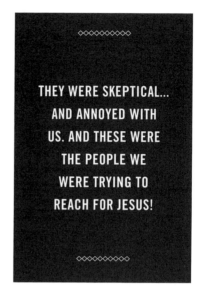

THEY WERE SKEPTICAL... AND ANNOYED WITH US. AND THESE WERE THE PEOPLE WE WERE TRYING TO REACH FOR JESUS!

The city, though, didn't have enough money to build the skate park. Billy showed me the article about it, and he then said, "We should build it for them." I didn't want to build their stupid skate park. They had turned down our plans to build, changed the zoning, and cost us tens of thousands of dollars in landscaping. I sure didn't want to do anything to help them! Billy could see what was going on in my head, but he didn't back off. He said again, "Greg, we should build it for them."

I barely mustered the conviction to respond, "Oh, all right." That was enough for Billy. He put everything in motion to contract for the excavation and the concrete. Before long, it was finished. The next article in the paper said, "Seacoast Donates Skate Park." It was the first positive article about us in a long time. (I took credit for the idea from then on.)

REVERSE OFFERING

This simple and inexpensive action planted a seed in my mind: we could do more, much more, for our community. We soon planned a "reverse offering." We took $10,000 out of our bank account, put in in small amounts in envelopes under every seat in the auditorium. I told our people, "This morning under your chair you'll find an envelope with some money in it. We took $10,000 of the money you've given, and we're giving it back to you. There's not much in each envelope, but it'll be plenty if you'll work together to make a difference. Now, if you need the money to make ends meet, take it and use it. But we're giving you this money so you'll trust God to multiply this $10,000 into at least $100,000 worth of good for people in our community. I suggest that you get together with your small group or some friends and ask God to give you ideas about how you can invest this money to bless other people. Here's what you can't do: You can't put the money back in the offering box next week. That's not the purpose. Be creative about how you can multiply the impact of this money, and then use it and see God work."

It was amazing. People came up with all kinds of great ideas. Some of them bought supplies for a lemonade stand and used the money they made to buy school supplies for kids in underprivileged parts of town. A businessman asked his small group to pool the money in their envelopes—it was only about $35. They bought a few square feet of wholesale flooring and sold it for a profit, used that money to buy more and sell more, and on and on. Eventually, they provided enough funds so that one out of ten flooring jobs at a particular company was a "Jesus job." Our church project lasted only a month, but this group keep it up for over a year, putting many thousands of dollars of flooring into people's homes.

> I BELIEVE IN DECEN-
> TRALIZATION. IF WE
> GIVE PEOPLE ROOM
> TO BE CREATIVE AND
> CELEBRATE THEM FOR
> GOING FOR IT,
> AMAZING THINGS
> INVARIABLY HAPPEN.

This wasn't a top-down project. I believe in decentralization. If we give people room to be creative and celebrate them for going for it, amazing things invariably happen. During this month, every person in our church was looking at the community through a different pair of eyes. They saw needs in people's lives I would never have seen, and God moved their hearts to care for people in tangible ways. Let me give a few examples: One small group pooled their money and bought supplies to put on a dinner. They charged for the meal and gave the proceeds to a homeless shelter. Another group pooled their money and built a handicap ramp for a family that needed one. Several kids bought ingredients for sugary drinks, set up a stand, and gave the proceeds to worthy causes.

A group of ladies bought supplies to make blankets for newborns who had extended stays in the local hospital (and they continue to do this today). An ongoing homeless ministry started as a result of this effort. The list of creative and generous actions is almost endless, and we were ready for even more.

PURPOSE-DRIVEN COMMUNITY

Rick Warren wrote *The Purpose-Driven Church* and followed it with the best-seller, *The Purpose-Driven Life*. I thought the natural next step would be "The Purpose-Driven Community." By this time, we had about 500 small groups. We asked each group to brainstorm about how they could have an impact on the people in the community, and we gave them six weeks to implement their plans.

I believed God wanted this effort to be much bigger than our church, so before we began, I talked to a half a dozen pastors from other churches and asked them to invite leaders from the city to come to an informational meeting. About 60 showed up, including pastors of churches from widely different denominations; black, white, and Hispanic; and a few who had been vehemently opposed to us building a bigger building. After I explained what Seacoast was going to do, I invited them and their churches to join us, and 35 signed up. As is my custom, I didn't give them a lot of direction. I told them to pray and ask God for creativity and wisdom, and they came up with plenty of innovative ideas.

At the end of the six weeks, we had Rick Warren come to preach and celebrate what God had done through our groups. We invited people from

Seacoast and the other 35 churches, and we met in a stadium. We had almost 10,000 people in the crowd, and they were so excited about two things: God had used them and they were going to hear from Rick Warren. All of this created quite a buzz in Mt. Pleasant . . . a positive buzz this time.

DANGEROUS

I read an article in *USA Today* about "The Most Dangerous Cities in America," and I didn't have to read far to see that North Charleston was Number 7 on the list. Charleston is a city of bridges, and they separate the different parts of the metropolitan area. North Charleston is only a ten-minute drive from our church, but it's a world away in terms of culture and security. As you drive into the city across the bridge over the Wando River, on the left you see the picturesque city of Charleston, what *Conde Nast* has said is one of the top tourist destinations in America, and on the right you'll see old factories, tenements, rundown neighborhoods, and the scene of addiction, drug pushing, and violence. For years, I looked only to the left, but on the day I read the article, my eyes went to the right. I sensed God whisper, "What are you going to do about that problem?"

My instant response was, "Nothing." We were doing multi-site, running great programs, planting churches, leading people to Christ, and all kinds of other good things. Hadn't we just led 35 churches in the "Purpose-Driven Community"? Our plate was full. And besides, our strength is in ministering to people in suburban communities, not a blighted inner city. I wanted to say, "God, they're writing about us in books. You ought to read some of them." But I couldn't shake the nudge of the Spirit.

A few weeks later, our leadership team was at a Leadership Network event in Dallas. I was riding in the car with our Mt. Pleasant campus pastor, Sam Lesky. The Lord had been putting Sam on my heart, so I turned to him and said, "Sam, God is calling you to North Charleston."

Sam is originally from a pretty rough part of New Jersey. As soon as I said it, tears came to his eyes, and he told me, "To be honest, I relate better to the people in North Charleston than to the people in Mt. Perfect." That was all the confirmation I needed. That afternoon I took Sam to a Western store to buy him a pair of boots to seal the deal of his opening a campus in North Charleston. (I'm not sure why boots seemed appropriate, but they did. I wanted to do something to celebrate the moment. It was his first pair of cowboy boots, and he still wears them proudly!)

Not long after we got back from Dallas, Sam met with the mayor, school superintendent, police chief, and other officials in North Charleston to ask them about their concerns and hopes for the city. We rented (and later bought) an old church building in the middle of the part of town that had the worst rates of addiction and crime. We wanted to do much more than have a traditional church there, so Sam and I went to Los Angeles to learn all we could about Matthew and Tommy Barnett's Dream Center.

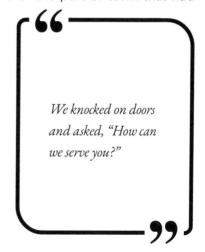

We knocked on doors and asked, "How can we serve you?"

When we came home, we started with the simplest strategy. We marked off 12 blocks and had Seacoast small groups "adopt a block" to show love to the people there, and we provided classes in English as a

Second Language. We knocked on doors and asked, "How can we serve you?" We tried our best to provide resources or connect the person with other organizations that could help. We always asked, "How can I pray for you?" and we prayed for the person or the couple or the family right then and there. At first, I'm sure the people wondered what we were doing in their neighborhood. They might have thought we were Jehovah's Wit-

nesses or politicians looking for votes. But after a few seconds of introducing ourselves and offering to serve and pray, people almost always opened their doors and welcomed us. Genuine compassion breaks down a lot of barriers. That day something needed to happen to redeem people from two different worlds—I sensed that we needed to be the tangible hands and feet of Jesus to meet the needs of those who could use some love, some encouragement, and some tangible resources. These were good people, many of whom hadn't had the opportunities that we had been given.

To get more ideas and inspiration, I talked to my friend Dino Rizzo and our team read his book, *Servolution*. He gave us a lot of fresh suggestions about how we could be more effective in connecting with people and providing genuine help. That's not always easy. Sometimes, well-meaning people actually hinder those they try to help by doing things for them they need to do themselves, so we had to gain wisdom to discern when helping was hurting.

When we started the church and Dream Center, we wanted to establish a medical clinic, but we didn't have the money. A man with resources visited the city. When we took him to North Charleston and explained the need and the opportunity, he caught a vision for a clinic. He provided the funds so we could buy the equipment and rent facilities. Doctors and other medical professionals volunteered their time, and it has been a fantastic success.

Let me give a few examples of how God has used the Dream Center. Each year, it . . .

- Distributes about 52 tons of food to disadvantaged families.

- Gives thousands of articles of clothing.

- Partners with seven other churches to provide 4,000 Thanksgiving dinners.

- Sponsors "Cinderella Day," providing hundreds of prom dresses, accessories, hair styling, and makeup for girls in high school.

In addition . . .

- The Dream Center Clinic offers primary medical care, as well as dental and vision care for 6,000 patient visits each year. The Clinic also provides 12 types of specialty care, including mammography, colon screening, skin cancer screening, and minor surgery.

- Our mentoring program, called E3, is training 78 at-risk students.

- The Dream House, in collaboration with Charleston Adult Education and SC Works, provides education and life-skills to low-country residents. Classes include GED prep, English as a Second Language, sound engineering, Dave Ramsey's "Financial Peace," and medical coding. A recent semester had 80 students enrolled and 20 on the waiting list.

- Our Friday Night Street Ministry gives 50 to 75 hot meals to people without a permanent residence, and we provide shower and laundry facilities on weekdays.

- We offer a Summer Lunch Program on weekdays for any student 18 and younger.

One of the most important ways we've been able to help people in North Charleston is by partnering with teachers and school administrators. At the time, the main high school was graduating only 36 percent of their seniors. This simple statistic is the driver for many of the woes of the community. People without diplomas either can't get work or get very low paying jobs, which results in poverty, which too often leads to drug addiction, gangs, and violence to lash out against any slight in search of some sense of identity and power. And the children of these people get caught up in the cycle and repeat it. Sam spearheaded a mentoring program for students. I wondered if I, or anyone I knew, could remember the basics of trigonometry. Sam told me that's not the problem. The kids needed something more basic and more important. They needed someone to be a

positive influence, to love them uncondition-
ally and be the voice of "more" in their lives.
Society and circumstances were telling them
what they could not be, what they could not
have, and what they could not do. We needed
to be the voice of more, the voice of yes, the
voice of Jesus. They needed people to represent Jesus' love and strength. The educational
part is easy; the loving part is foundational.
We wanted to follow these kids for a year.

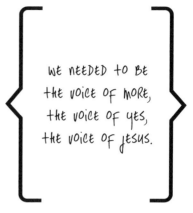

We needed to be the voice of more, the voice of yes, the voice of Jesus.

We started with six; we now have 100 adults mentoring students in the
high school. Among those we mentor, the graduation rate is 87 percent.

I think God is using us to make a difference. The police chief told Sam that
we're not the only reason, but we're one of the reasons the crime rate has
dropped significantly in that part of North Charleston. That's an identifiable
sign that God is using us to make a difference.

The reputation of the Seacoast campus in North Charleston is diametrically
opposite of the one we had before we built the skate park. City officials
and the media are thrilled to have us there. Their support opens a lot of
doors for us to do even more good in the community. But we haven't forgotten the mission of evangelism and discipleship—it's all woven together
in a beautiful fabric. Today about 1000 people worship in that little church
building in the center of North Charleston.

A left-leaning newspaper in Charleston publishes a "best of" list every year:
the best restaurants, the best hotels, the best beaches, the best B&Bs, the
best museums, and on and on. Almost every year, our church is cited as the

best church in the area. Of course, they get in a little dig by describing us as "the best McFranchise church." That's fine. In fact, their affirmation means even more because they also say, "No matter what you may think about churches, this one is making a real difference in the community." That's a long way from what the papers said about us years ago!

All of this began when Billy Hornsby had the idea of building a skate park for the city, and even though at the time I wasn't exactly the biggest supporter of his idea, I'm thrilled to see where that single step has eventually led us. All of these activities have given us a wide door of opportunity (see Colossians 4:3) to interact with thousands of unchurched people, and by the grace of God, many of them have come to faith. There is no conflict between our heart for evangelism and our efforts in social justice to care for the poor. As in the ministry of Jesus and the early church, the two go hand in hand. Some pastors assume a great band and sharp visual effects are the main ways to attract unbelievers, but I believe visitors are much more impressed when they see us caring for people who have nothing to give in return. That makes them sit up and notice . . . and sit down and listen. Today, pastors often talk about their "brand." The brand of Jesus was His compassion, and ultimately, His willingness to give everything for ungrateful people. I want that to be the brand of Seacoast, too.

IN THE FACE OF EVIL

In June of 2015, I was in Montana on a fishing retreat with a group of pastors. Cell phone reception was spotty at best. On Wednesday night of the 15th, a man on our safety team, who is connected with the police departments in the city, texted me: "There's been a shooting in downtown Charleston, and we think it's at a church." A few minutes later, he sent another text: "It's definitely at a church. There are fatalities." The next text said, "It's Mother Emmanuel." Mother Emmanuel is the name people have given Emmanuel African Methodist Episcopal Church since it's the "mother church" of the denomination. I had met their pastor, Rev. Clementa Pinkney, who was also a state senator, and I had his cell number. I called him, but I got no answer. I texted him, "If there's anything Seacoast can do, let me know," but I got no response. I had no idea he was dead. The man who had originally contacted me texted again: "There are multiple fatalities. I think you should get back here as soon as you can."

I caught flights back to Charleston the next day. By the time I arrived, the police had apprehended the shooter, Dylann Roof, in North Carolina. He admitted to the crime, and he explained that he meant to ignite a race war.

The arraignment was scheduled for Friday, and the police chaplain called and asked me to be there. At that point in our nation's history, a number of young black men had been killed by police in cities throughout the country, and some of those communities erupted in protests and violence. This could be even worse, and we had no idea how people would react, black or white. If Seacoast hadn't been involved in caring for so many people in the city, I don't think I would have been on the list of pastors the chaplain called. But by then, I was seen as a spiritual father for the city. It was a high privilege and a heavy responsibility.

The courtroom is small and cramped, and the air conditioning didn't seem to be working very well at all. Soon after I arrived, family members were escorted into the courtroom and sat in the few available seats. With only about 50 chairs, the room was packed with family, reporters, and officials. In fact, it was so small that they allowed only two or three family members for each of the nine people who had died.

I was part of another crowd of people outside the courtroom. I was wearing a suit and sweating profusely, but that wasn't the problem. My mind was racing trying to figure out what to do. I settled on one key question: "What would Dino Rizzo do?" He'd find a way to serve instead of just sitting there. I asked someone to run out and buy a case of water. When he came back, I gave bottles of water to anyone who wanted one.

A few minutes later, the chaplain suggested I go into the courtroom to offer water to the family members. When I asked what I could get them, one of them said, "I'd like a Diet Coke."

"No problem. I'll be back."

I found one of our staff members in the waiting room, and I said, "Quick! Go somewhere nearby and find a Diet Coke. Bring it back as soon as you can."

Only a few minutes later, I took the Diet Coke to the person who had asked for it. It felt so good to be able to do that simple act of kindness for someone who had lost so much.

As I walked toward the door, the chaplain motioned for me to stay in the room. It was so crowded that the only space I could find was against the back wall. Two attorneys stood on either side of me. As they talked, I could sense the solemnity of the moment. Through television cameras, the whole world was watching what was happening in Charleston.

The judge called the arraignment to order, and Dylann Roof appeared on a large video screen from a secure location in the jail. CNN showed a full-screen picture of Roof during the proceedings, but it didn't show anyone in the courtroom. The judge asked the families if they wanted to make an impact statement. The daughter of one of the murder victims stood up. Through her tears, Nadine Collier, the daughter of shooting victim Ethel Lance, told Roof, "You took something really precious away from me, I will never talk to her again, never hold her again, but I forgive you. You hurt me, you hurt a lot of people, but God forgives you and I forgive you."

Bethane Middleton-Brown, the sister of one of the victims, stood up and said to Dylann Roof, my sister "taught me that we are the family that love built, we have no room for hate, so we have to forgive. And I pray to God for your soul, and I also thank God I won't be around when your judgment day comes with Him." [1]

Anthony Thompson is the pastor of another church in Charleston, but his wife was killed in the Bible study that night at Mother Emmanuel. He took the opportunity to speak: "You've taken the very best from me. I choose to forgive you, and if you'll bow your knee to Jesus and confess your sins, the rest of your days can be your best days." Anthony was the one who was instrumental in inviting black pastors to participate in our citywide "Purpose-Driven Community" outreach. When the arraignment was over, we hugged each other and cried.

That remarkable day, I saw nine families choose to forgive one of the most horrible acts of evil I've ever known. That tragic night, Roof didn't just walk

---

1   "Affidavits spell out chilling case against Dylann Roof," Yamiche Alcindor and Doug Stanglin, *USA Today*, June 19, 2015, https://www.usatoday.com/story/news/nation/2015/06/19/dylann-roof-charleston-police-charged--murder-black-church/28975573/

into the church and start shooting. He came to the Bible study, sat and bowed his head through the prayers, and only when he had been warmly accepted among them did he pull out his .45 and begin shooting those who had prayed with him just moments before. During all the statements of heartfelt forgiveness, the attorneys standing next to me kept looking at each other and mouthing, "This is unbelievable!" "This is unreal!"

A question struck me: if this event had happened at a Bible study at Seacoast Church, would the nine families choose to forgive only two days after their loved ones had been murdered? I hope so, but I don't know. I concluded that I didn't care if Rev. Clementa Pinckney's theology or politics lined up with mine or not. This man had led his people to experience a depth of God's love, forgiveness, and grace that revolutionized their lives and enabled them to forgive a young man who killed purely out of hate. The hearts of the people that day said more about their pastor and their church than anything else possibly could. When Rev. Pinckney hit the floor that night and entered the presence of Jesus, I'm sure the first words he heard from the Savior's lips were, "Well done, good and faithful servant. Enter into the joy of your Master!"

> **A question struck me: if this event had happened at a Bible study at Seacoast Church, would the nine families choose to forgive only two days after their loved ones had been murdered?**

Before the arraignment, I had asked a lot of people to pray about what might happen. Depending on the statements, the city could go up in flames and we could have blood in the streets. That's not overstating the risk. In the previous year, the news had carried images about many other cities where people were outraged by injustice. In Charleston, something very different happened: Dylann Roof went to the Bible study to spark a race riot, but a revival broke out instead. Over the next few days, black people and white people hugged each other, sang and prayed together, and loved each other. At one point, Anderson Cooper of CNN was broadcasting from the streets. During an interview, he stopped the conversation, turned to the camera and said, "You've got to hear what's going on behind me." A group of people were singing "Amazing Grace."

On June 20th, the day after the arraignment, 20,000 people from all over the country came together to march across one of the bridges leading into Charleston. They called it "The Bridge to Peace." Symbolically, two groups started at opposite sides of the bridge, met in the middle of the span, joined hands, and stopped for nine minutes of silence to honor those who had been killed. An ABC affiliate reported, "The marchers also prayed, cheered and sang. There were high fives and hugs. Cars along the bridge and boats traveling below showed their support by honking. The marchers chanted together, declaring, 'We are Charleston strong.' The group was led by members of the victims' families, alongside Charleston police chief Carl Ritchie."[2]

Some hard days were coming up quickly. Mother Emmanuel was going to host nine funerals after virtually all of their pastoral staff had been killed — and the entire world was watching. My friend Tim Scott, U.S. Senator from South Carolina, called and explained that in the African-American culture, meals are served at funerals, and he asked us to help. A young mom, Stacey Gregory, was in the church office when we got Tim's call. She leads a group called Missional Mothers, using play dates with their kids to reach out to other moms and include them in the fun, which then opens

2   "Thousands march across Charleston bridge in powerful display of unity," *ABC*, June 22, 2015, https://abc7ny.com/society/thousands-march-across-charleston-bridge-in-display-of-unity/798730/

doors to conversations about the Lord. When she heard about the need, she immediately told me, "Our small group will take care of the meals."

I shook my head and smiled, "There's no way. Do you have any idea how many people are going to attend these funerals?"

She told me confidently, "We'll do it. We'll figure it out."

For some reason, I believed she could do it...and she did. She enlisted the help of other moms and created a viral sensation of people who offered to bring tons (literally tons) of food. I have videos of SUVs opening their back doors and unloading container after container of delicious food, some home cooked and some catered by restaurants, for the funerals over the next few days. There were about a thousand people at most of the funerals, but 5,000 at Rev. Pinckney's funeral. President Obama gave a moving eulogy at the service.

That day, the protesters from Westboro Baptist Church showed up to inflame hatred in the name of Jesus. Some men in our church gathered a large group to form a barrier between the Westboro protesters and everyone who had come to mourn Rev. Pinckney. Our men performed an unsung and unnoticed service, but it was as important part of what made the day so meaningful to so many.

Only days later, the new leaders of Mother Emmanuel wanted to start the Wednesday night Bible study again. That morning, I went to the church and saw bullet holes in the walls and the furniture. In the evening, about 200 people came to hear God's Word and pray. Stacey didn't want to be left out. She and her amazing team of moms brought food for that night, and they kept bringing food to the Bible study for the next year. In appreciation, she was inducted into the Mother Emmanuel Women's Auxiliary. It was the highest and most meaningful honor anyone could give her.

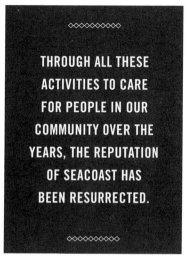

THROUGH ALL THESE ACTIVITIES TO CARE FOR PEOPLE IN OUR COMMUNITY OVER THE YEARS, THE REPUTATION OF SEACOAST HAS BEEN RESURRECTED.

In the aftermath of the tragedy, as the funerals ended, the Bible study began again, and the family members continued to grieve, the administrative people at Mother Emmanuel became overwhelmed with calls, emails, and letters. They didn't have a computer system, and most of their staff was no longer in place. A lady who was trying to run their church office called and asked if we'd meet with her. When we found out the scope of the need, we formulated a plan to help. People donated computers, and we set up an office at Seacoast to handle their correspondence. Day after day, they brought us boxes full of mail. My assistant, Kathy Roseborough, organized the effort. We had about ten volunteers come to our office every day to open mail and record information. Mother Emmanuel wanted to send thank-you notes to everyone who had been so kind and served them so well, and this was a way we could help them. Kathy and her team of volunteers spent about ten months working through all the correspondence.

Through all these activities to care for people in our community over the years, the reputation of Seacoast has been resurrected. Our people are incredibly innovative and dedicated to meet the needs they uncover. I don't think we deserved all the criticism we received years ago when the paper regularly trashed us, and we don't deserve all the credit we get today...but it's a lot more fun to read the paper now!

WATCH FOR IT

Our efforts beyond the walls of our church began as a corrective—to make a statement to the community leaders that we weren't as bad as they thought we were. That may not be the most noble of motives, but it's the truth. Over time, however, God worked in us to provide many opportunities to demonstrate the compassion of Jesus in a hurting world. Here are some principles I've learned:

*** BEWARE OF tunnel vision ***

Your church began because someone, maybe you, had a vision to reach the community, but over time, it's easy for the strains of running a church to absorb our attention. Sooner or later, our "outreach" is only hoping unchurched people will come to us, and we don't do much to go find them. Exhausted leaders care more about retention than extension. Our vision can become very limited. When I've heard pastors talk about their people serving, some of them are thinking only about what happens within their walls. God's purposes are far bigger than that!

*** LEAD WELL, BUT DECENTRALIZE ***

Years ago, I read a fascinating book, *The Starfish and the Spider*. The authors, Ori Brafman and Rod Beckstrom, use those animals as metaphors of two kinds of organizations. If you cut the head off a spider, it dies, but if you cut a leg off a starfish, it has the innate ability to regenerate. In other words, if an organization relies too much on its CEO, president, or pastor, it becomes fragile and vulnerable, but if it decentralizes, each segment of the organization can grow, develop, and thrive. A church has to have at least a little bit of spider to provide clear direction, but many pastors make the mistake of being too centralized in planning and implementation, robbing their people of the joy of being creative and seeing their ideas change lives. We've cultivated a starfish culture at Seacoast. Fairly often, people in the community tell me about something "Seacoast has done," and I didn't know anything about it. Our people don't wait for me to inspire them, direct them, or resource them. They see needs and dive in to meet them.

Our role as leaders at Seacoast is to figure out how we can create and maintain a starfish culture, and then find ways we can support our people as they take the initiative to care for people. The role of the leaders is to continually keep the eyes of our church focused outward. We also coordinate our church's relationships with partner organizations so the people at Seacoast can serve effectively in them. Of course, some individuals and small groups want to create opportunities on their own. That's fantastic, but most people prefer a range of existing options where they can choose to serve. As leaders, we set the vision, provide possibilities, and inspire people to love others like Jesus loves them.

✱✱✱ RESPOND tO CRiSES ✱✱✱

The most important role in a crisis is to just show up and provide a shoulder to cry on. But we need to understand some cultural nuances that can make people willing to accept our help. For instance, in the

African-American community, people dress up for special occasions, like church, court, and funerals. If I'd gone to the courtroom for the arraignment wearing my normal blue jeans, I would have been disrespectful. I wore a suit to show my respect and to earn the privilege of giving family members water and a Diet Coke.

Tim Scott helped me understand the importance of providing meals at the funerals, and God provided Stacey Gregory to orchestrate the incredible generosity and love to serve meals at those important events.

Serving in the community isn't an add-on to the purpose of the church. It's central. God has called all of us to serve the body of Christ within the walls of the church, the people in need in our communities, and at least to some extent, the people throughout the world. We can't do everything in those three areas, but we can do something.

*** BE KNOWN AS A GIVER, NOT A TAKER ***

God has created us to make a difference. If we'll open our eyes to see the people in our communities, we'll notice needs we've overlooked for years. And as we meet them, God will let us see even more. As we've experienced the transforming love of God, we'll love the people Jesus died for—including those who have different values, different politics, different ethnic backgrounds, and different life stories.

- If you're planning to plant a church, make it part of your strategy from the beginning to reach beyond the walls of your church to have a loving presence in the community.

- If your church is young and growing, don't take it for granted that people will come to you. Keep reaching out to touch people in need so your people will realize that's a crucial part of following Jesus.

- If your church has grown stale and you need to relaunch a vision, it's very easy to focus on the internal systems: better music, leadership development, and all the other things inside the church—including handling the criticism of people who aren't happy with your leadership! In a relaunch, go back to the Great Commission and the Great Commandment. Build into the plan a robust outreach in the community. Invest resources to make a difference there, and watch how God transforms the culture of your church.

- If your church is going great guns, you're probably already outward focused. Keep it up, and inspire the starfish among you to be innovative in caring for people who can't give anything back.

Other pastors and other books have a more detailed strategy for serving the community. I encourage you to read their books and follow their advice. All I can tell you is to love God, keep looking at the people He loves, decentralize to inspire creativity, and celebrate what God does through your church.

1

What are some obvious signs a pastor and a church are ingrown? What are signs they're outward focused?

....

....

....

....

....

....

....

2

Do you need to allocate more resources (and your attention) to make a difference in your community, or are you investing plenty there already? Explain your answer.

....

....

....

....

....

....

....

THINK ABOUT IT

3

What are the groups
of people in need in
your community that
your people are already
caring for? How can you
support these care-
givers and provide more
resources for them?

....

....

....

....

....

....

....

....

4

For you and your
church, what's the right
blend and balance of
being a spider and being
a starfish?

....

....

....

....

....

....

....

....

....

5

Is your church known for
being a giver or a taker?
Explain your answer.

....
....
....
....
....
....
....
....
....

6

What has God said to
you in this chapter?

....
....
....
....
....
....
....
....
....
....

CHAPTER SEVEN

WHEN YOU HIT THE WALL

Q: WHAT KEEPS YOU GOING WHEN YOU FEEL LIKE GIVING UP?

In one way or another, all pastors have been in Isaiah's shoes when God asked, "Who shall I send?" and he answered, "Here am I. Send me!" For many, that was a glorious moment of divine presence; for others, it scared us to death. The point is that we, however reluctantly, answered the call. When we read stories of leaders in the Bible, we quickly realize God took them through crucibles of suffering as well as giving them times of success.

It is inevitable, I believe, that sooner or later every leader comes to a point of despair. It may happen because the leader has made a bone-headed decision, when there is unfair opposition, the economy turns south and there's not enough money to pay the bills, a family crisis arises, or any number of other reasons. Young pastors need to be warned that this day of reckoning is coming; older pastors have already faced their share of them, but it's easy to be caught off guard again. In these painful moments or long seasons, we hit a wall. We wonder, "How did I get into this mess? God, did you really lead me here? What in the world do I do now?"

I've had many of these instances. One of the first ones happened on my inaugural mission trip to India with my son, Jason. We flew to Mumbai where we had an eight-hour layover. We booked a hotel room so we could get some sleep, and I paid for a prepaid taxi ride. I didn't know, however, that we landed in the middle of a strike by taxi drivers.

Our flight landed at 2:00 in the morning. Both of us were utterly exhausted and desperately needed the sleep. I changed some dollars to rupees so we had at least a little money in case we needed it. When we walked out to the curb to get our taxi, I quickly discovered we would have to make other arrangements. There were rides available, but they weren't the city-sanctioned cars and drivers. They were people who were only too happy to nod and take my money when I gave them the hotel address. The first one drove us to an empty parking lot and motioned for us to get out. The next one took us a little farther into the parking lot. After a while, we'd taken several rides, but we were still in the dark and forbidding parking lot. Jason and I weren't making much progress, but they were making a lot of money. I'm not the quickest person in the world, but it didn't take long to figure out that they saw us as easy marks. I prayed, "God, did you send us to the other side of the world so we could die in an airport parking lot?" I hit the wall that night. I've already described other occasions when I hit a wall as a pastor. Perhaps the biggest was when the city council zoned our area so we couldn't build a bigger building. That seemed like an insurmountable, impenetrable wall.

NOT WHAT THEY EXPECTED

The church in Antioch commissioned Paul and Barnabas to take the gospel to what is now central Turkey. On their first stop in Cyprus, they encountered a magician named Elymas who tried to distort their message and confuse the proconsul who was listening to their message of grace. What was Elymas's angle? If the proconsul believed in Jesus, he wouldn't have any need for a magician any longer! Paul wasn't shy. Luke tells that Paul . . .

> . . . filled with the Holy Spirit, looked straight at Elymas and said, "You are a child of the devil and an enemy of everything that is right! You are full of all kinds of deceit and trickery. Will you never stop perverting the right ways of the Lord? Now the hand of the Lord is against you. You are going to be blind for a time, not even able to see the light of the sun."

> Immediately mist and darkness came over him, and he groped about, seeking someone to lead him by the hand. When the proconsul saw what had happened, he believed, for he was amazed at the teaching about the Lord. (Acts 13:9–12)

I can imagine Barnabas watching all this and shouting, "Booyah! That's what I'm talking about!"

Paul and Barnabas then sailed to Pisidian Antioch where they attended the synagogue. Visiting religious leaders were usually asked to speak, so they gave the floor to Paul. He explained that Jesus was the fulfillment of all the promises and all the prophets. They had been waiting for a Messiah, and Jesus had come! He is the king they had longed for. Many of those who were listening believed, and they invited Paul and Barnabas to come back the next Sabbath. That day, "almost the whole city gathered to hear the word of the Lord" (Acts 13:44), but the Jewish leaders were jealous and opposed Paul's teaching. The Gentiles in the crowd celebrated, but the Jews caused such anger that they drove them out of the city. Still, "the disciples were filled with joy and with the Holy Spirit" (Acts 13:52).

This stop had been a study in contrasting reactions to the gospel. The next two would also demonstrate diametrically opposite responses. In Iconium, they again went to the synagogue to speak, and many people, both Jews and Greeks, trusted in Christ. But this time, the opposition by the Jewish leaders "poisoned their minds against the brothers." Paul and Barnabas stayed to continue their outreach, performing miracles and preaching the gospel, but when the leaders threatened them with bodily harm, the two evangelists fled to Lystra.

The reception in Lystra was overwhelmingly positive . . . way too positive! When Paul and Barnabas arrived, Paul healed a crippled man. When the crowd saw the man walking, they shouted, "The gods have come in human form!" They drew some conclusions about the two men: "Barnabas they called Zeus, and Paul they called Hermes because he was the chief speaker. The priest of Zeus, whose temple was just outside the city, brought bulls and wreaths to the city gates because he and the crowd wanted to offer sacrifices to them" (Acts 14:11–13).

I don't know about you, but I appreciate it when people give me affirmation. The extravagant display by the people in Lystra was meant as a great honor for Paul and Barnabas, but that's certainly not how the two men interpreted what was happening! They tore their robes in horror and rushed into the crowd to assure them that they weren't, in fact, gods, but they were proclaiming Jesus, the real God. The people were so amazed at their power to heal that they still had to be restrained from offering sacrifices to Paul and Barnabas.

In John's Gospel, he says that Jesus did so many more things than he recorded that all the libraries in the world couldn't hold the descriptions.

We get the same idea in the next scene. With an incredible economy of words, Luke tells us that the people in Lystra did a 180: "Then some Jews came from Antioch and Iconium and won the crowd over. They stoned Paul and dragged him outside the city, thinking he was dead. But after the disciples had gathered around him, he got up and went back into the city. The next day he and Barnabas left for Derbe" (Acts 14:19-20).

Some pastors are blindsided by struggles and opposition they encounter. They believe that their commitment to serve somehow earns them the right to consistent growth and the appreciation of those they lead.

Some pastors are blindsided by struggles and opposition they encounter. They believe that their commitment to serve somehow earns them the right to consistent growth and the appreciation of those they lead. That would have been news to Paul. In city after city, he hit walls of opposition, but in city after city, he wasn't surprised. He knew that when Jesus called him, He meant that we would suffer opposition, setbacks, and even slander...because servants aren't better than their Master.

Paul's experiences in this brief look at the beginning of his first missionary journey weren't isolated. Trouble was his middle name! When others tried to discredit him to the Christians in Corinth, Paul gave them a list of his "credentials" as a servant of Christ:

> I have worked much harder, been in prison more frequently, been flogged more severely, and been exposed to death again and again. Five times I received from the Jews the forty lashes minus one. Three times I was beaten with rods, once I was pelted with stones, three times I was shipwrecked, I spent a night and a day

> in the open sea, I have been constantly on the move. I have been in danger from rivers, in danger from bandits, in danger from my fellow Jews, in danger from Gentiles; in danger in the city, in danger in the country, in danger at sea; and in danger from false believers. I have labored and toiled and have often gone without sleep; I have known hunger and thirst and have often gone without food; I have been cold and naked. Besides everything else, I face daily the pressure of my concern for all the churches. Who is weak, and I do not feel weak? Who is led into sin, and I do not inwardly burn? (2 Corinthians 11:23–29)

Very few of us, in this country at least, encounter this kind of opposition. Our frustrations, however, are very real to us, even if they're not as severe as Paul's. We struggle with what God brings or allows in our churches, team relationships, finances, health, marriage, and kids. Our reputations seem very fragile. We feel demoralized when someone flames us on Facebook and when a trusted friend talks behind our backs.

Sometimes, problems come from out of the blue. When we prepared to launch Seacoast, God led me to the perfect building. We were so excited that we sent out a mailer a month before the grand opening to almost 20,000 households saying, "Save the date! Seacoast Church is having its first service!" The week after the mailer went out, the fire marshal came to inspect our building. When he finished, he told me bluntly, "You can't meet here. It's not ready." He rattled off a list of changes and upgrades we'd have to make before we opened. Remedy was utterly impossible. I had to find another place for us to meet.

I went to schools, warehouses, and every other place that might hold several hundred people. Nobody would let us meet there. Elation only a few days before had turned to gloom. On a rainy day, I was driving around looking for somewhere (anywhere!) we could meet. I felt so hopeless that I pulled over and stopped the car. The windshield wipers kept slapping back and forth. Between wipes, I noticed that I had parked in front of a theater. I hadn't asked them yet! Nobody goes to the movies on Sunday morning—I hoped. The manager agreed, and that's where we held our first service for Seacoast. The setback at the building where we planned to launch the church became part of Seacoast's story because God showed up and provided a way.

NEVER FORGET

When we come to a point when we've hit a wall, we need to remember a few fundamental truths:

*** GOD HAS TRUSTED YOU WITH A POWERFUL MISSION. ***

Problems can overwhelm us. They cloud our minds, rob us of optimism, and create strongholds of doubt in the depths of our souls. When we're going down the tube, we need to hold on tight to the fact that

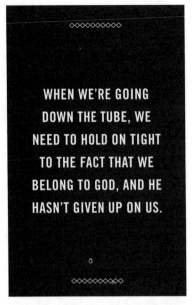

WHEN WE'RE GOING DOWN THE TUBE, WE NEED TO HOLD ON TIGHT TO THE FACT THAT WE BELONG TO GOD, AND HE HASN'T GIVEN UP ON US.

we belong to God, and He hasn't given up on us. In his letter to the Ephesians, Paul reminds us, "For we are God's masterpiece. He has created us anew in Christ Jesus, so we can do the good things he planned for us long ago" (Ephesians 2:10 NLT).

You aren't junk, and you aren't disposable—you are the product of God's masterful creation, a work of art, cherished by God. And we didn't get into all this on our own. On the night He was betrayed, Jesus made sure His disciples understood the importance of the right perspective. He reminded them, "You did not choose me, but I chose you and appointed you so that you might go and bear fruit—fruit that will last" (John 15:16).

You were created for significance. It's easy to go from the highs of seeing God use us to the lows of feeling useless and alone. Failure, criticism, unforeseen twists in the road, and a hundred other factors can erode our confidence in God's calling. We remember how God used us, but those days seem like a distant dream. No matter what has happened to bring you to this point, God still has something for you. God didn't give up on Abraham for lying about his wife to save his own skin, on Moses for being reluctant to stand up to Pharaoh, on Jacob for deceiving everybody but his mother, on Peter for betraying Jesus, or on you and me. If you have a pulse, God's work through you isn't finished, but remember this: you can only accomplish your God-given mission by trusting in the power of the Holy Spirit. John encourages us, "You, dear children, are from God and have overcome [demonic powers], because the one who is in you is greater than the one who is in the world" (1 John 4:4).

*** THERE WILL ALWAYS BE PEOPLE WHO DON'T GET IT. ***

In Lystra, Paul and Barnabas ran into two kinds of people: those who thought too much of them and those who thought too little of them. As we lead our churches, some people give us too much credit. They may not want to sacrifice bulls in our honor, but they're too quick to ascribe to us God's power to change lives. When God uses pastors to bless the world, some people who are watching mistakenly exalt the pastors to the place of God.

One of our jobs as leaders is to root out hero worship before it begins... and nip it when we notice it taking root. We do this by being real. Like Paul and Barnabas, we need to tell our people that we're just like them, with the same temptations and many of the same struggles they face.

But the problem with hero worship isn't all "them"; it's often "us." We want to take credit for what God has accomplished. We bask in the glow when our kids are doing well, and we feel crushed when they struggle. Yes, they are shaped by both nature and nurture, but I've known far too many Christian leaders who have loved their kids like crazy but their children didn't turn out to be paragons of virtue and faith. Actually, I think the kids we get are the luck of the draw. We can also take credit for our intellect, our wit, our talents, our money, and our looks. (We look in the mirror and conclude, "Man, God was having a good day when He made me!" Or in the words of the great philosopher, Zoolander, "Some of us are just ridiculously good looking!") In conversations, we subtly (or not so subtly) draw attention to ourselves, and we make sure people are well informed about our part in the growth of the church. If we're going to be successful in our mission, we can't be a slave to the praise of people.

It is innate in all of us to point to our accomplishments, to boast in what we think is worthy of attention and fame. Through Jeremiah, God reminds us of the only thing worthy of our boasts:

> This is what the LORD says:
> "Let not the wise boast of their wisdom
>   or the strong boast of their strength
>   or the rich boast of their riches,
> but let the one who boasts boast about this:
>   that they have the understanding to know me,
> that I am the LORD, who exercises kindness,
>   justice and righteousness on earth,
>   for in these I delight,"
> declares the LORD. (Jeremiah 9:23–24)

What do you and I boast in? Our smarts, our physical or oratorical power, or our wealth and comfort? The only thing worth boasting about is that we experience the presence and power of Jesus, and we value the things He values. That's all that really counts. Everything else is a distraction.

Paul and Barnabas encountered a second kind of people: those who threw rocks at them! When the Jewish leaders in each city heard Paul speak, they were convinced that Jesus was outside the teaching of the prophets. And they didn't disagree agreeably! When we lead, we can expect opposition—it comes with the territory. It's striking to me how early in the gospels the writers tell us that the religious leaders wanted to kill Jesus! The people in your church and your community hopefully don't want to kill you, but they often resist bold new plans.

When Seacoast was getting started and was attracting the unchurched, we made some people feel uncomfortable. Some started spreading another name for us, "Seacult." At one point, an investigative reporter from the left-leaning newspaper in the city called and asked for an interview. He said the paper was releasing an article the next week, and he wanted to give me a chance to tell my side of what he'd discovered. He came, and I answered his questions. I hoped for the best, but I wasn't stupid. The next week, this newspaper was all over town with a huge picture on the front of me speaking . . . and an image of me on the screen behind me. The headline read: "The Growing Cult of Seacoast: Why thousands of young adults are flocking to the Mt. Pleasant church." The article, however, wasn't as scathing as the headline. The conclusion was that our theology is sound but our services have a modern twist. And after doing a lot of research about me, the reporter concluded I'm not an egomaniac and I wasn't siphoning money from the church for my personal gain (which makes me wonder why he labeled us a cult . . .).

One person wryly observed, "It's easy to tell the pioneers. They're the ones with arrows in their backs!" I wonder how often Paul remembered that he had been the chief opponent of Christians in the earliest days of the church. He understood that the Jewish leaders felt threatened because this new faith had at first threatened him by its popularity and growth.

Only the newest pastors are surprised by opposition. Those who have been around a while fall into two camps: those who have learned to expect it and are prepared when it comes, and those who have been badly burned and now avoid opposition by never boldly leading their churches. Choose Option A.

*** WHEN CiRCUMSTANCES OR PEOPLE HAVE KNOCKED YOU DOWN, GET UP AND KEEP GOiNG. ***

The people of Lystra were a fickle bunch. They wanted to make Paul and Barnabas into gods, but then they stoned Paul and left him for dead. In a remarkable scene in the life of the great apostle, he got up and went back into the city! Man, if I woke up from being stoned by a crazed mob, I sure wouldn't go back!

I've known pastors who weathered betrayal by a staff member with grace and wisdom, but they were devastated by a financial crisis. And I've known pastors who were crushed by a family problem but handled other difficult situations fairly easily. The point is that different stresses may get our goats, but different causes can lead to the same result: feeling utterly stuck and without a way forward. We need to remember that we're not alone.

> "
> *The point is that different stresses may get our goats, but different causes can lead to the same result: feeling utterly stuck and without a way forward. We need to remember that we're not alone.*
> "

• Thomas Edison's teachers said he was "too stupid to learn anything." He was fired from his first two jobs for being "nonproductive." As an inventor, he made 1,000 unsuccessful attempts to make a working lightbulb. A reporter asked him, "How did it feel to fail 1,000 times?" He responded, "I didn't fail 1,000 times. The lightbulb was an invention with 1,000 steps."

- Albert Einstein didn't speak until he was four years old, and he couldn't read until he was seven. His parents believed his intelligence was "sub-normal," and one of his teachers described him as "mentally slow, unsociable, and adrift forever in foolish dreams." He was expelled from school and was refused admittance to the Zurich Polytechnic School. He eventually learned to speak and read, and he wasn't too shabby in math.

- Henry Ford went broke five times before he succeeded.

- R.H. Macy failed seven times before his store in New York finally began making a profit.

- Daniel Boone was asked if he had ever been lost in the wilderness. He thought for a moment and replied, "No, but I was once bewildered for about three days."

- Walt Disney was fired by a newspaper editor because he "lacked imagination and had no good ideas." He went bankrupt several times before his drawing of a mouse changed everything. When he proposed building a park in Anaheim, California, the city rejected it because officials were sure it would only attract riffraff.

- Jerry Seinfeld's first onstage appearance at a comedy club was a disaster. He looked at the audience and froze. He finally stumbled through about "a minute and a half" of material, and was jeered off the stage.

- Dr. Seuss's first book, *To Think That I Saw It on Mulberry Street*, was rejected 27 times by publishers. [1]

In *Failing Forward*, John Maxwell advises us to look at failure through a new set of lenses:

- People think failure is avoidable. It's not.

- People think failure is an event. It's not.

- People think failure is objective. It's not.

- People think failure is the enemy. It's not.

- People think failure is irreversible. It's not.

- People think failure is final. It's not.

In fact, Maxwell notes that entrepreneurs fail an average of almost four times before they succeed.[2] Many people would consider me an entrepreneur, and I was fired three times before I saw much progress in my

---

1   Cited in several sources, including "Thoughts on Business Communication and Other Oxymorons," October 19, 2007, https://cootelibeau.wordpress.com/page/17/

2   John Maxwell, *Failing Forward* (Nashville: Thomas Nelson, 2000), pp. 13–16.

career. The last pastor who fired me told me, "You need to go back to work for Hewlett-Packard because you have no future in ministry." We can experience many setbacks, but we don't fail until we stop getting back up and trying again. A Texas proverb says, "It doesn't matter how much milk you spill as long as you don't lose your cow." [3]

> none of his problems that Luke records in Acts, even being stoned and left for dead, was the end of his story. Every time, he got up.

The kingdom of God is upside down: the last shall be first, we gain life by losing it, the way to greatness is to serve, we experience love and acceptance when we admit we're broken and sinful, and strength is perfected in weakness. Suffering was inherent in Christ's calling, and as we follow Him, suffering will inevitably come our way. Paul explained the principle to the Corinthians:

> But we have this treasure in jars of clay to show that this all-surpassing power is from God and not from us. We are hard pressed on every side, but not crushed; perplexed, but not in despair; persecuted, but not abandoned; struck down, but not destroyed. We always carry around in our body the death of Jesus, so that the life of Jesus may also be revealed in our body. (2 Corinthians 4:7–10)

I'm especially encouraged that Paul admitted he was sometimes perplexed. I don't know how often that happened to him, but it happens a lot to me. In all of his struggles, the opposition he experienced, and the loneliness he felt, Paul kept moving forward. None of his problems that

---

3   Ibid., p. 15.

Luke records in Acts, even being stoned and left for dead, was the end of his story. Every time, he got up.

NEVER ALONE

When we read the account of Paul being stoned in Lystra and him getting up and going back into the city, it's easy to overlook one of the details in the story: he got up "after the disciples had gathered around him" (Acts 14:20). One of the most common—and the most destructive—ways we respond when we hit the wall is to isolate, to assume no one will understand, and live in self-imposed relational exile. In times of heartache and discouragement, we need to reach out to friends even more, not less. And when people we love have hit the wall, they may act like they don't want us around. Don't believe it for a minute. Give them some space, but make sure they know you're present, you care, and you're not going to give simplistic answers to life's biggest problems.

Don't be shocked when you face seemingly insurmountable obstacles. They're either already here or they're coming—count on it. You're going face times in leading people when you want to quit. You're going to realize you've tried to do ministry in your own strength. You'll figure out that you've boasted in your own talents instead of God's greatness and grace. Some of the people around you will put you on a pedestal and praise you instead of God. Get down and stay down. And some will give you a gut punch. Take it and keep going. To the Galatians Paul gave encouragement all of us need:

> Let us not become weary in doing good, for at the proper time we will reap a harvest if we do not give up. (Galatians 6:9)

In my first pastorate in Freeport, Illinois, I thought I had all the answers. (It was the not-so-logical conclusion of a young man who had previously been fired three times from roles as youth pastor and was taking over a church where 13 people had voted on my candidacy.) That first week, we had Sunday morning, Sunday evening, and Wednesday evening services. In my life to that point, I had preached three messages to adults, and now the people in Freeport had already heard everything I had to say to them. My gun was out of bullets. I was done. In the second week, it snowed so much that drifts were halfway up the front door of the church. I could have called the custodian, but that was me. I could have called an administrator, but that was my job, too. They had told me the church had problems when it rained hard, so as soon as all this snow melted, I had to deal with flooding inside. I had been there only two weeks, and already I thought, *This isn't what I signed up for!*

The snow gave me a reprieve from having to come up with three new sermons, but week three was coming up fast. I found something to say in each of the three services that week. To be honest, the Wednesday nights were awful. Only the diehard crazy people came those nights...the good thing is that there were only six of them, but the bad thing is that this meeting sapped the life out of me. Not too long after we moved to Freeport, I became depressed—the kind of depression that you can't find the strength to get out of bed all day. After a while in this pit of darkness, God sent my Dad, some passages from His Word, and an encouraging book to give me a new perspective and lift my spirits. The book is one by Robert Schuler. He wrote that the greatest churches in America hadn't been founded yet, and there might be someone in the Midwest who could plant one of these churches. I hoped he was talking about me! I claimed his words as prophetic.

I believe Schuler's words are still true: the greatest churches on the planet are still to come, and God has entrusted leaders all over America and the world with a powerful mission...leaders like you.

Do good. Make good repeatable. And don't give up.

DO GOOD.

MAKE GOOD
REPEATABLE.

&

[DON'T GIVE UP.]

THINK ABOUT IT

1

When was the first wall you hit as a leader? What happened? How did you cope with it?

....
....
....
....
....
....
....

2

What are some principles we learn from Paul and Barnabas in Lystra? How will these principles help you face difficulties?

....
....
....
....
....
....
....

3

What causes us to
forget that God has
entrusted us with a
powerful mission and
a powerful identity?
What happens when we
remember it's true?

....

....

....

....

....

....

....

....

....

....

....

....

....

....

....

....

....

....

....

4

Do you think Paul
was ever surprised by
opposition? Why or why
not? Are you? Explain
your answer.

5

Why is it a danger—for them and for us—for people to put us on a pedestal and give us too much credit for changes in people's lives and the growth of the church?

....

....

....

....

....

....

....

....

....

....

....

....

....

....

....

....

....

....

....

....

6

Over the years, what have you learned from failure that has made you a wiser, kinder, stronger leader?

....
....
....
....
....
....
....
....
....
....
....
....
....
....
....
....
....
....
....

7

What are three steps
you're going to take as
a result of reading
this book?

....

....

....

....

....

....

....

....

....

....

....

....

....

....

....

....

....

....

....

....

ACKNOWLEDGEMENTS

The support and encouragement of those I love are woven through every story, every principle, and every application in this book. I want to thank . . .

DEBBIE
The love of my life and biggest cheerleader. You make our story better.

KIDS AND GRANDKIDS
Jason & Jenna, Josh & Lisa, Josh & Jessica, Ben & Jenny, Miles, Addison, Everleigh, Greta Kate, Sadie, Rylan, Emorie, Judah, Southerlyn, Breck, Kingston, Eliza, Ellie & Esther. I love this crazy world we call family where chaos is normal and love is abundant.

TEAM SEACOAST
I'm grateful to our church family, some who have walked with me on a 30-year journey of God's amazing grace. I'm thankful for the team that works behind the scenes to provide an environment that's easy to grow in.

I'm especially grateful to those who have served me closely and made me look better than I am: Debbie, Becky, Joan, Kathy and Jenny. Your reward in heaven will be great!!

TEAM ARC

I'm thankful for the men and women who selflessly give so we can help so many leaders discover and reach the dream in their hearts. Any list would be too short. I'll never forget that day the dream became reality in Clinton, Louisiana, with Chris, Rick, Dino, Scott, Billy and Ms. Gayle. Sometimes the reality grows bigger than the dream.

SUSAN BLOUNT AND PAT SPRINGLE

You made this process a delight. I think we make a pretty good team. Maybe we should do this again someday.

TERRY

Friends really are friends forever.

GRANDMA SURRATT

I'm glad you raised your hand. Your decision continues to change generations.

ABOUT THE AUTHOR

Photo by Kim Graham @kimgrahamphoto

Greg Surratt is the founding pastor of Seacoast Church, which was planted with the goal of reaching unchurched people in the Charleston area. Greg led Seacoast as it grew from one campus to many, as Seacoast became one of the first churches to pioneer the multi-site approach to the weekend experience.

Greg is the president and co-founder of the Association of Related Churches (ARC), which is a global church-planting initiative that has established over 800 churches worldwide since its founding in 2000.

He is the author of the book *Ir-rev-rend: Christianity without pretense, faith without façade*, as well as a contributor for *Outreach Magazine*, *Ministry Today Magazine*, and *Charisma Magazine*.

Greg is married to his childhood sweetheart, Debbie, and together they have 4 children and 14 grandchildren. He enjoys photography, fishing, golfing, and rooting for the Cubs, Broncos and Gamecocks.

DEBBIE AND ME
WITH OUR GRANDKIDS

Association of Related Churches

We are a global family of church and business leaders that exists to see a thriving church in every community reaching people with the message of Jesus. We do this by providing relationships, resources, and opportunities to leaders of new and existing churches so that they can thrive.

WE LAUNCH

We have a highly successful, proven model for planting churches with a big launch day to gain the initial momentum needed to plant a church. We train church planters, and we provide a tremendous boost in resources needed.

WE CONNECT

We provide dozens of opportunities to connect with other church planters, veteran pastors, leadership mentors, as well as friends who are walking the same path as you are. You're never short on opportunities to connect!

WE EQUIP

Our team continually creates and collects great ministry resources that will help you and your church be the best you can be. As part of this family, you get to draw water from a deep well of experience in ministry.

AUNCHING, CONNECTING, & EQUIPPING THE LOCAL CHURCH

ARCCHURCHES.COM   @*ARCCHURCHES*   */WEPLANTLIFE*

ADDITIONAL RESOURCES

**TO ORDER COPIES OF *SERVE YOUR CITY*,
*SERVE YOUR CITY SMALL GROUP
LEADER'S GUIDE AND PARTICIPANT'S GUIDE*,
GO TO ARCCHURCHES.COM**